Twayne's English Authors Series

EDITOR OF THIS VOLUME

Sarah W. R. Smith

Tufts University

Gerald Griffin

TEAS 307

Gerald Griffin

GERALD GRIFFIN

By ROBERT DAVIS

Harborfields High School
Greenlawn, New York

TWAYNE PUBLISHERS

A DIVISION OF G. K. HALL & CO., BOSTON

Copyright © 1980 by G. K. Hall & Co.

Published in 1980 by Twayne Publishers,
A Division of G. K. Hall & Co.
All Rights Reserved

Printed on permanent/durable acid-free paper and bound
in the United States of America

First Printing

Frontispiece of Gerald Griffin by F. W. Wilkin
Original in Christian Brothers' O'Connell Schools, Dublin

Library of Congress Cataloging in Publication Data

Davis, Robert, 1930–
Gerald Griffin.

(Twayne's English authors series; TEAS 307)
Bibliography: p.146–49
Includes index.
1.   Griffin, Gerald, 1803–1840—Criticism and interpretation.
PR4728.G8Z59   823'.7   80-18427
ISBN 0-8057-6799-1

For Karen, Bradford, and Kari

Contents

About the Author

The author is teacher of English and Humanities at Harborfields High School in Greenlawn, New York. After receiving his doctorate in English at New York University, he taught at Manhattanville College in Purchase, New York and C. W. Post Center of Long Island University. Presently he is working on a book on Charles Lever, another nineteenth-century Irish novelist.

Preface

The aim of this book is to identify Gerald Joseph Griffin as a nine-teenth-century Irish regional novelist who dramatized in his prose the lives and times of his people, the peasants and middlemen of Gaelic Munster, Ireland, in the eighteenth century and in the opening decades of the nineteenth century.

In treating Griffin's identity and purpose as a writer in chapter 1 and the history of eighteenth-century Ireland in chapter 2, I believe that the examination of his prose works, which follows, will be better under-stood in terms of a man who feared that the creation of highly believ-able characters, such as Hardress Cregan in his best work *The Colle-gians,* would be morally detrimental to himself and to his reading public. I have studied Griffin's novels and the single extant example of his dramatic writing, *Gisippus,* to show how his propensity to preach denied him the full realization of his artistic potential. It is the dra-matic structuring of his scenes and the social verisimilitude which his peasants deliver that receive close attention, for in these two features of Griffin's writing are found the value of an artist who believed that his primary function was to teach a moral.

This study of Griffin's works seeks further to provide insight into a relatively unknown period in Irish history and Irish culture. His char-acters, from crusty Kerry hillmen and sheep stealers to half-sirs and members of the British garrison, testify to Ireland's disorder from early Penal days to those of the Great Liberator, Daniel O'Connell. The effects of one nation's usurpation of another, of one artist's blinking, then fading before the social chaos that was his milieu, are of one piece in the works of Gerald Griffin.

Griffin was born on December 12, 1803, in the city of Limerick, Ireland, to middle-class Roman Catholic parents. When he set out for London nineteen years later to revitalize the English stage, as he thought, to return it to classicism by means of his plays, he did so at a time when English restrictions against Irish Catholics, the Penal Laws of the eighteenth century, were being relaxed. As one of the first of Ireland's novelists, Griffin brought to his English readers a subject about which they knew relatively little, a record of the lives of Irish-men living in Munster, the southern province of Ireland. His writing was solidly based on the history of Ireland, particularly the history of the eighteenth century, and it bore the indelible mark of a man of deep religious convictions who wanted to write perfectly moral books. Throughout his entire career Griffin published little that was not of a thoroughly didactic nature. However, for all of his moralism he knew how to entertain. History, drama, story, humor, characterization, setting, as well as moral instruction often combine in his early writing to offer clear insight into a paradoxical culture.

Gerald Griffin wanted to write morally perfect novels. When he failed, he decided to live, as best he could, a morally perfect life. His piety, genius, and profound sense of Ireland's past led him quite naturally to the overall theme of reform. His moralism stemmed from an unalterable sense that his people, the Catholic peasants, who constituted four-fifths of the population of Ireland in the third decade of the nineteenth century, must be directed to the practice of forgiving and forgetting so that individuals could be made whole and national unity and identity achieved.

With one kind of ambition, a desire for fame and success, Griffin began his writing career. But his writing taught him his true vocation—service to God as a member of the religious order of the Christian Brothers. In his writing he could not fail to evoke history; and when he did he discovered his mission in life was not art but religion, not writing but teaching the poor the meaning of their lives. Griffin wrote didactically because his people's ignorance lay in their "unacquaintance with the ordinary duties of Christian citizens and with the arts necessary to constitute as well as adorn civilized society."[1] The precise purpose of the Penal Laws was to obliterate Irish Catholic identity, and the fact that this failed was due mainly to the preservative effects of an outlawed religion. Griffin, inspired by the history of the peasants' sacrifice and endurance, began to write about this "army" who would outlive the law that sought their destruction.

Griffin was essentially a solitary person throughout his life, yet he cherished the company of his immediate family and a few close friends. The anonymity he insisted upon as he sought success in his early London experience from 1823 to 1827 contrasted sharply in 1829 with his fame as the author of *The Collegians*. Griffin as an anonymous man had to succeed through his own merits as a writer, but when he did succeed he felt compelled through scruples to give up his successful formula—the presentation of ruling passions in the lives of his characters. When he finally entered the novitiate he wrote to a clergyman:

"I have not yet known what it is to regret the world. If I regretted anything it would be that we had not sooner parted. If those who enter religion late in life fail not to receive some of the peace which it confers, what must it be to the young who give it their morning and their noon with all the freshness and vigour of their early affections."[2]

The solitariness of Griffin's life is contrasted with its public aspect, with the kind of effort he put into most of his work: he preached for the solidarity of his people and for an awakening to a glorious national heritage. To him the contemporary Irish political scene meant confrontation with British authority and the whole socioeconomic framework of landlord control of the lives of Ireland's peasantry. The spirit of the natural rights of man had seized this peasantry under the inspiration and leadership of Daniel O'Connell, who was sent to the British Parliament by their vote. Griffin was reacting creatively to his people's inchoate struggle for emancipation when he wrote his last two novels, *The Invasion* and *The Duke of Monmouth*.

Gerald Griffin was too much a perfectionist in Christian living to place literary fame before the dictates of his conscience. Moreover, his profound sense of history told him what his people needed most from his life—the best possible example of Christian living. Other factors preying upon his conscience, forcing him into religious retirement, were his premonitions of an early death, experienced almost from childhood, and the severe attacks of palpitations of the heart, which began during his years in London. His love for Mrs. James Fisher indicates still another reason for retreat to a monastery. They were close friends for nearly a decade, and toward the end of Griffin's public life he wrote these lines:

> Was he selfish?—not quite; but his bosom was glowing
> With thronging affections, unanswered, unknown;
> He looked all round the world with a heart overflowing:
> But found not another to love like his own.[3]

Griffin fits conveniently into the eighteenth century and the tradition of the didactic English novel. He is also one of the first Irish Catholic novelists to write preponderantly in a moralistic vein. John Cronin says Griffin's "cultural roots" are "stuck somewhere in Pope and Goldsmith. . . . On the other hand, as a regional novelist, he belongs with Scott and Banim."[4] He is also the first Irish Catholic novelist to faithfully represent the peasant and the middleman of southern Ireland.

Art and didacticism were of one piece in the works of Gerald Griffin until a moral paralysis ended his art at a point in his career clearly marked by success and promise. Griffin's art ended because, as he told his brother and biographer Daniel, he could not feel justified in creating "in his own breast all the passions of that character even for the moment."[5] This moment arrived after the publication of *The Collegians*, his best work, in 1829 when the author was twenty-six years of age. He was never again to create a character of such effective moral force and beauty as Hardress Cregan, for, when Griffin refused to oppose his scruples in the creation of characters, he denied himself a deeper knowledge of himself as an artist as well as a greater verisimilitude in his art. The works which followed this resolution to resist what had become tantamount to an occasion of sin, the creative act, are mediocre; nevertheless, they indicate the potential which had been abandoned. What becomes increasingly clear to the reader of Griffin's works is that the writer's decision to avoid passion in the creation and representation of characters is also his plea to his readers to avoid passion in their lives.

Griffin's peculiar temperament, his developing attitude toward Ireland and to literary aesthetics, and his early decline must be discussed within this study of the man and his works. Isolate the moral aspect of his works and an ineffectual preacher emerges; isolate his comic best and he is merely flattered. Distortion of one kind or another will find its way into the evaluation of Griffin unless he is treated comprehensively. Thus, this study will attempt to differentiate between the works of Griffin which succeed and fail according to the measure with which his scrupulosity gripped his art.

When the moral lesson, Griffin's chief concern in writing, failed to eclipse the artistic values of dramatic structure, characterization, and tragicomedy, then Griffin's writing was at its best. Some of his early tales were beautifully balanced pieces: art and morality complemented one another. Other tales of his early work bore obvious signs of hasty construction and crude didacticism, but the latter seems in the minority. The rapidity with which Griffin wrote *Tales of the Munster Festivals* (1827), for example, and the arduous conditions under which he wrote them explain their weaknesses, but the *Tales* clearly demonstrate his genius.

Griffin's works involve his probing, moral consideration of the various social planes of Irish life filled with fragmented loyalties and ancient hatreds. As artist, moralist, and national prophet he presents the lives and destinies of Munstermen who endured Penal days, hoped for emancipation, and dreamed of freedom and sovereignty. The structural unity of this Munsterman's writings, his brilliant comedy so intrinsically a part of the social tragedy he presented, the moral force and beauty of his early characterizations all combine to render Irish character and tradition, to record a culture. An anonymous writer for the *Dublin Review* in 1844 expressed the sentiment that a country, Ireland in this case, must have in its literature a nationality.[6] For the "complicated and self-contradictory society"[7] that was Ireland in the first decades of the nineteenth century, Griffin created an identity. By equating his characters with national purpose—unity and peace in Ireland—he became a social evaluator, a prophet, a guardian of his people's destiny.

Space does not permit consideration of Griffin as a poet and journalist. However, sufficient commentary does exist within the text to suggest the significance of both of these facets to a writer whose primary mission in life was to win his soul to God.

I am grateful to G. P. Putnam's Sons for permission to quote from Ethel Mannin's *Two Studies in Integrity*. To Professor William A. Fahey I owe thanks for his assistance in a variety of ways. I am indebted to Professor David H. Greene whose wisdom and knowledge have been most inspirational. The assistance of Dorothy Walker and the staff of the Northport Library remains a blessing. My wife Karen Kaasa Davis receives my love and devotion for making all things possible.

ROBERT DAVIS

Northport, New York

Chronology

1803 Gerald Griffin born in Limerick on December 12, son of Patrick and Ellen (Geary) Griffin.

1810– Life at Fairy Lawn. Education ends.
1820

1820 Patrick and Ellen Griffin, with several of their children, sail for America. William, Daniel, Gerald, Ellen, and Mary Anne settle in Adare.

1823– London experience as playwright, hack, and novelist.
1827

1827 *Holland-tide; Tales of the Munster Festivals.*

1829 *The Collegians.* Meets James and Lydia Fisher.

1830 *The Christian Physiologist; The Rivals and Tracy's Ambition.* Begins to see less of Lydia Fisher. Pallas Kenry his chief residence.

1832 *The Invasion.*

1835 *Tales of My Neighbourhood.*

1836 *The Duke of Monmouth.*

1838– Joins the Christian Brothers. During his Dublin novitiate he
1840 refuses to see Lydia. Dies of typhus at Cork Monastery on June 12.

1842 *Gisippus* successfully produced at the Drury Lane Theatre for the entire season. *Talis Qualis.*

1843 *Poetical Works.*

CHAPTER 1

Griffin's Identity and Purpose

D ANIEL Griffin's biography, *The Life of Gerald Griffin by His Brother* (1842), has been the source for most of what has been written about the life of this Irish novelist; Ethel Mannin's *Two Studies in Integrity: Gerald Griffin and the Reverend Francis Mohoney ('Father Prout')* adds but a few notes based mainly on unpublished letters Mannin found at the Christian Brothers' monasteries in Dublin and Cork.[1] The facts about Gerald's life on the whole are few, but what appears most significant is that the writer chose to abandon the success formula he discovered in writing *The Collegians* so that he could attempt to write perfectly moral books. Beyond the scope of what has been written previously about this Irish novelist, the following biographical sketch and, to some extent, this study of his works attempt to speculate on the role Lydia Fisher played in his life and his writing.

I Fairy Lawn

Patrick Griffin, Gerald's father, left farming in County Clare to manage a brewery he had purchased in the city of Limerick. Construction of a townhouse accompanied the venture, and it was during this interim of managing and building that Gerald, Patrick's ninth son, was born. As Gerald grew within the bustle and excitement of his family's traffic, only his brother Daniel came to know him on an intimate basis. Anyone wishing to know Gerald during these formative years in Limerick and later at Fairy Lawn had to approach him with the idea of becoming intimate. Even before his family he maintained diffidence with charm, calm with pride. His deep affection for his family never was understood fully by its members during this period spent in Limerick simply because of the intensity of their activities and the awesome antics of a father who knew less about operating a brewery than he did about farming in Clare.

When the brewery business failed through mismanagement, Patrick sold their new home and moved the family to a lovely site twenty-eight miles west of Limerick. Here he built another dwelling from plans he himself designed. He called their new home Fairy Lawn, and no doubt the magic of the name and the beauty of the surrounding countryside bordering the magnificent estuary of the Shannon River excited the already sensitive and responsive imagination that Daniel noted earlier during the first seven years of Gerald's life in Limerick. What Gerald found at Fairy Lawn was the freedom and beauty of nature to which he trusted the precious and private thoughts of his spirit for symbols of expression. He found also the history of his country, the destroyed monasteries and castles of medieval Ireland, and having combined the images of nature and of ruins, he wrote, for example, as a very young man, the following lines, taken from his poem "Matt Hyland":

> Thou rushing spirit, that oft of old
>   Hast thrilled my veins at evening lonely,
> When musing by some ivied hold,
>   Where dwelt the daw or martin only;
> That oft hast stirred my rising hair,
>   When midnight on the heath has found me,
> And told me potent things of air
>   Where haunting all the waste around me.[2]

Fairy Lawn, where Griffin spent ten happy years as a child (1810–1820), is approximately one quarter of a mile east of Loghill, a hamlet close by the Shannon's shore on the road from Limerick to Tarbert. A sharp acclivity conceals the original structure which is now owned by a farmer whose name, O'Connor, is coincidentally, the same as that given by Griffin to the family who occupied a home in a similar location in "Touch My Honour Touch My Life," a tale from *Tales of My Neighbourhood*.

Patrick Griffin wanted his wife and large family to be comfortable in their new home, and the spacious, single-storied building, now completely refurbished and modernized, is just that. From any one of their four spacious windows facing north, the O'Connors enjoy the same view celebrated by the Dalys in their breakfast scene in *The Collegians*.

Behind Fairy Lawn for thirty miles the uplands of western Limerick roll to the valley of the Blackwater. From these hills the *Abha bhan* rushes through a gorge where as a boy Gerald often fished, dreamed, and stored impressions he recreated later in prose and verse. Two miles from Fairy Lawn is the glen of the Ovaan, a stream which empties into the Shannon at Loghill. The glen itself contains a small chapel which once served as a school and was attended by Gerald. In all probability it is the model for the chapel desecrated by Dinny MacNamara in "Suil Dhuv" from *Tales of The Munster Festivals*. The glen and the surrounding area of castle ruins, decayed big houses, dilapidated homes of squireens like Hyland Creagh of *The Collegians*, mud cabins of peasant farmers and the swarms of homeless and starving peasants set upon by evictions and famine in 1821 were all a part of the land that Griffin knew so intimately. Its lore and violence emanated from the enforced injustice of the few who controlled the soil and wealth of Ireland.

In this neighborhood of castle and church ruins, Gerald was impressed with one thousand years of history. For example, four miles to the southwest is Shanid, a site where in 839 the Norse were defeated by Gaelic warriors whose feat probably inspired the work of Elim, the hero of Griffin's *The Invasion* who turns back a similar Norse invasion. The ruins of Shanid Castle, dating back to the beginning of the thirteenth century, mark the site of the earl of Desmond's first seat and are celebrated in a poem by Griffin, entitled "Shanid Castle." Through its verse Griffin corresponds with a time quite similar to his own in which Ireland lay in degradation.

II   A Note on Genealogy

Genealogist M. Mohoney notes that Gerald's grandfather, James Griffin, is buried five miles east of Loghill "at a ruined church of Enoc Padraig above his Corgrig home, in a great vault which his family shared with their neighbours, the Bourkes of Tiermore."[3] Mohoney reveals that Griffin's surname does not appear among Limerick landowners in the Desmond or Cromwellian surveys but that this Clare branch of the family probably held considerable tracts of land before the Cromwellian Plantation. Egan O'Rahilly, the Gaelic poet (1670–1726), says Mohoney, "has some vigorous lines on a conforming Murtagh Griffin who acquired property and influence in Kerry about 1700, and the poet makes it clear that this Griffin was a newcomer from Clare. . . . The Nash-Griffins of Kerry were Protestant and early in the eighteenth century two brothers, Frances and Richard, married two Fitzgerald sisters, granddaughters of a Knight of Kerry. A descendant

of a third brother was the Right Reverend Dr. Griffin who preceded
Dr. Graves as Protestant Bishop of Limerick."[4] This blend of Protestant
and Catholic in Griffin's background no doubt contributed a great deal
to the writer's tolerance and conservatism, for in all that he wrote the
just man triumphs regardless of religious affiliations. His resolution for
life and art was that differences be settled peaceably, that Christian
charity prevail.

III   *Griffin's Education*

The solitude and privacy of Gerald's Fairy Lawn home sponsored
his romantic fancy as well as his recollection of the past. Nature
crowded in on him and with her the young poet communicated. However, there had to be a time for formal education, and this discipline
came to the boy in the form of private tutors at Fairy Lawn, none so
celebrated as Richard MacEligot who gave Gerald his first lessons in
Limerick. Patrick John Dowling writes of MacEligot, in his chapter
dealing with teachers of the "city academies," as being "self-taught,
pursuing his work with such zeal and industry as to attain a high
degree of proficiency in the subject he set out to teach; his knowledge
of   the   native   language   and   literature   was   considerable   and
scholarly. . . ."[5] MacEligot, and those of his kind, usually tutored small
groups of boys in Latin and Greek, in addition to the more common
subjects of reading, spelling, arithmetic, and penmanship. At Fairy
Lawn, Gerald progressed to the study of French and the classics of
English literature. In the latter realm, the youth received great impetus
and direction from his mother Ellen who urged particularly upon the
boy the works of Goldsmith.

Ellen Griffin was apparently a devoted wife and mother. To her husband and ten children she gave herself completely and unselfishly. To
Gerald she imparted her enthusiasm for the moral aspects of literature.
Throughout the remainder of her life she continued to urge the young
man to continue his devotion to virtue and charity. As a result of this
early influence, Griffin was never free to create passion in the lives of
his characters but once, and that occasion—the writing of *The Collegians*—ended his career as a successful novelist. Ellen Griffin's contribution to Gerald's life and his art was her moral sensitivity, her appreciation of moral beauty in life and art. Patrick Griffin, Gerald's father,
appeared to be as whimsical as his "new life" starts suggest. He was
relaxed in business as he was in the privacy of his home, and his humor
and cheer made all about him quite comfortable. Of great importance

to Gerald as writer was the fund of lore and history that Patrick imparted to his son. His stories and those from the peasants with whom Gerald spent a great deal of time provided the novelist with an unfailing sense of his people's feelings and imagination.

As a member of the Irish Volunteers Patrick had shared the pride of the thousands who defied the British in 1782 and regained for Ireland her legislative freedom. Gerald's own interest in politics as well as his awareness of national origin began, no doubt, as he came to understand the talk of his father and older brothers on the subject of French, English, and Irish national affairs, as the talk brought the history of eighteenth-century Ireland closer to the present moment.

Within the ten years that Gerald spent at Fairy Lawn, his love of nature and literature sprung to life, his "formal" education ended, and his identity as a middle-class Munsterman came to include an intimate knowledge of the Munster peasant. Of greatest importance to the future writer, however, was the fact that Fairy Lawn had provided the environment in which the child could indulge his sensitivities and imagination in complete privacy and communion with river, mountain, stream, and meadow and yet return to the warmth and balance of a family in touch with the world at large. Perhaps a good example of the results of such early experiences lay in the fact that Griffin supported wholeheartedly O'Connell's movement for Catholic emancipation while he condemned the violence perpetrated by peasants against oppressive landlords, tithe proctors, and clergy. Griffin knew how the peasants were exploited, but in no way other than through the courts did he sanction the correction of injustices. Since there was little justice under British law for the Irish peasant, Griffin dramatized in his tales the point that, until Irishmen were fairly treated in their own land by British authority, there was little hope for lasting peace.

IV *Loss of Parents*

From Fairy Lawn Gerald's parents left for America in 1820. Patrick's eldest son had discovered the promise of a new nation while serving as an officer with the British army and persuaded his father to leave Ireland and her difficulties for the blessings offered by a homestead in Susquehanna County, Pennsylvania. The parting left Griffin with a profound sense of loss compounded by his trials in London as a hack writer and never compensated for by his passion for writing. This same sense of loss was relieved for a short time in his relationship with Lydia Fisher and finally abated in the last eighteen months of his

life as a member of a religious order. Reflections of this separation from
his mother appeared in his writing for years to come. One of the earliest is in an introductory sonnet to his second series of *Tales of the
Munster Festivals*, 1827:

> That home is desolate!—our quiet hearth
>   Is ruinous and cold—and many a sight
> And many a sound are met, of vulgar mirth,
>   Where once your gentle laughter cheer'd the night.
>   It is as with your country; the calm light
> Of social peace for her is quenched too,
>   Rude discord blots her scenes of old delight,
> Her gentle virtues scared away, like you:
>   Remember her, when in this Tale ye meet
> The story of a struggling right-of ties
>   Fast bound, and swiftly rent-of joy-of pain—
>   Legends which by the cottage-fire sound sweet,
> Nor let the hand that wakes those memories
>   (In faint, but fond essay) be unremembered then.

In these lines are some of his earliest themes drawn from his own
observation of the social chaos which had surrounded him during his
years at Fairy Lawn but from which he was able to withdraw into a
wild glen or deserted spot near a huge cliff. These are a few of the
themes which expressed his deep sense of personal loss and his acute
awareness of the suffering and disruption in the lives of his
countrymen.

Personal grief and social awareness, fusing early in Griffin's writing
career, reached a climax in *The Collegians*. Here the mother-son relationship seems a curious reversal of that which he had shared with his
own mother. The moral about the ruin a possessive and vain mother
can produce in her relationship with her son is obvious, but a sense of
Griffin's own resentment in respect to his separation from Ellen Griffin
works its way to the surface. Griffin's hero-villain, Hardress Cregan,
passionately denounces his mother's way, while a reader can suspect
that in this book, published one year before Ellen's death in 1830, Griffin is quite unconsciously upbraiding his own mother for her departure.

V   *Adare*

From Fairy Lawn the Griffins—William, Daniel, Gerald, Ellen, and
Mary Anne—moved to Adare, a village ten miles west of Limerick.

Here in Adare Gerald's literary ambition was born. In this charming setting where the road from Limerick southwest to Killarney crosses the River Maigue, Edwin, third earl of Dunraven (1812–1871), fashioned this ideal village. Adare Manor, situated in a beautifully wooded demesne on the west bank of the Maigue, was built in Tudor style from 1831 onward and served as Griffin's model for the home of Lord Peppercorn, in "The Great House," from *Tales of My Neighbourhood* (1835). The demesne adjoins the village and contains, among its quiet scenes of undulating grounds overlooked by huge oaks and elms, the ruins of a fifteenth-century Franciscan friary, church, sacristy, cloister, and cemetery. These religious ruins deeply affected Gerald. The spirit of piety and religious exercise he drew from them prompted a passionate, literary response mostly in imitation of Virgil, his favorite author at the time. However, the most profound effect of his love for such surroundings was felt only later by Brother Gerald Joseph Griffin, when he revealed that only through a religious life did he think he would ever save his soul.

From Adare Gerald now began to travel often to Limerick as a member of a "Thespian Society." He, with a few other amateurs and a few professionals, wrote plays and performed in them for local charities. John Banim had been writing reviews of the Thespian Society's productions when he was not in London seeing to the production of his own plays. Thus, the two met to begin a relationship that was to mean much to Griffin a few years later in London when he so desperately needed guidance and encouragement as a young playwright. Banim, later to be hailed as the "Scott of Ireland" for his brilliant work in characterizing the peasant of the province of Leinster in his *Tales by the O'Hara Family*, had been admired by members of Griffin's family at Fairy Lawn for his letters to the *Limerick Evening Post* signed "A Traveler," and so it was with extreme pleasure that Gerald wrote to his family in America that he was on familiar terms with this rising dramatist of the London stage.

VI *Anonymity*

During this theatrical interlude Griffin first manifested his antipathy for notoriety. One member of the society had submitted a bit of literary criticism to a Limerick newspaper under an assumed name. Shortly after the piece appeared it was severely attacked by another unknown critic. Gerald's friend and partner came to him for assistance and the two prepared an answer. The upshot of the whole affair was that Ger-

ald had written the scathing attack but rather than reveal himself con-
sented to answer his own criticism incognito. According to Daniel, Gerald's actions were in no way meant as a practical joke. This desire for
anonymity at a time when he was seeking self-assurance and acclaim
was a part of a growing tension: he was attempting to gratify the
wishes of the public and the private voice of his conscience which
addressed him on matters of service to his God, to his art, and to his
country. Perhaps through anonymity Griffin felt that he might be better able to withstand the shocks of reflection and disapproval that
might come his way.

VII   *Pallas Kenry*

Before Gerald left Ireland at the age of nineteen to follow Banim's
example as a playwright for the English stage, Dr. William Griffin
moved the family to the village of Pallas Kenry, six miles north of
Adare and two miles from the Shannon.

With William's consent, Gerald set off for London in 1823, bringing
with him a few pounds, several manuscripts, and a great deal of confidence and never dreaming that he would soon become a London
hack as he struggled to get his plays produced. The London stage in
1823 was ripe for reform, thought Gerald, and as spokesman for the
return of classicism, he was sure he would be heard. He could hardly
have imagined that fame would reach him as a novelist, nor that less
than two years after his death the only play that remained among his
manuscripts, *Gisippus*, would be performed at the Drury Lane Theatre for an entire season with the leading actor of the day, William
Macready, in the title role. His immediate failure in London, however,
drove him into greater seclusion and self-absorption.

VIII   *Griffin's London Struggles*

Instead of returning to Ireland or perhaps continuing his struggle,
with financial assistance from a family that could afford to be helpful,
Griffin became stubbornly independent as promises of assistance from
new acquaintances proved fruitless. Only one party seemed to warrant
Griffin's continued trust, John Banim, who was very helpful in provid-
ing connections for his friend; however, no good resulted until Griffin
struck off on his own, making some headway with several essays he
supplied to one editor under a pseudonym.

At this time Griffin's sensitivity at the shabby condition of his wardrobe drove him to refuse Banim's offer of an introduction to Dr. Maginn, a principal writer for *Blackwood's Magazine*, who could introduce the young Irishman to the editor of the *Literary Gazette*. Thomas Flanagan characterizes Dr. William Maginn as one from a group of Irish writers "Tory in politics and alienated in every sense" from both islands, but nevertheless responsible for encouraging the writing of the four books which created the nineteenth-century concept of Ireland:[6] *Tales of the O'Hara Family*, by John and Michael Banim; *Today in Ireland*, by Eyre Evans Crowe; *Fairy Legends and Traditions of the South of Ireland*, by Crofton Croker; and *Tales of the Munster Festivals*, by Gerald Griffin. Approximately two years later, after he had anonymously submitted samples of his writing to several editors and received some positive responses, Griffin did accept Dr. Maginn's introduction and was successful with the essays and articles about London life that he began to submit to the *Literary Gazette* as well as to several other magazines.

Griffin was still far from literary success even with more assignments than he could handle from London journals. Banim's advice and help deepened their friendship, but Griffin was still unwilling to supply Drury Lane with battle scenes, burning forests, or cataracts of real water and his efforts to get his plays accepted met with continued failure. Griffin was resolved to see his poetry upon the stage, and Banim opened doors to business associates and helped the young author revise his plays scene by scene. However, continued failure to get any of his dramas produced was beginning to suggest to him more strongly than ever before that poetry was banished from the stage.

At this point, Griffin nearly lost Banim's friendship. After two years of struggling as a hack, Griffin had begun to sustain himself by supplying copy for a number of major literary journals. Banim's *Tales by the O'Hara Family* had appeared and was successful; Griffin was now asked by his friend to contribute to the series in which it had been published. Banim was not making the offer merely out of charity; he knew his friend's talent. However, Griffin refused the offer because he abhorred patronage and because he was severely embarrassed about his state of affairs. An estrangement followed lasting nearly two years. When the two were finally reconciled, mostly through Griffin's efforts at accepting full blame for the misunderstanding, neither one could explain satisfactorily his behavior to the other.

Perhaps Griffin's success hastened the reconciliation—*Holland-tide* had been published in 1827 and Griffin was anxious to bestow copies of his first prose work upon his friend John Banim. Some success as a journalist and a parliamentary reporter, assigned by a London publication to the British House of Commons, had given Griffin the time and the means to devote himself to this first venture into a new genre. Since a curious British reading public wanted to know more about Ireland's agrarian unrest and the people involved in it, Griffin obliged, and so immediate was the success of his first book, which took Griffin three months to complete as he continued to write for the journals, that the young author plunged himself into the production of his second, *Tales of the Munster Festivals*, which required only four months to finish.

The *Tales*, he told his brother William, should be "Catholic": "they must represent the Catholic religion as it really exists among the clergy and the people, and not give such caricatures of it as are too commonly found in most of the writings of the day."[7] At this point in his career, only about three years after he had left his home in Ireland at the age of nineteen, Griffin was combining art and morality to produce some of his best writing. The proper balance was being struck between art and didacticism, or more precisely, art and representation of the Catholic religion.

To a large extent nationalism was an outstanding feature of the moral tone in Griffin's works. In 1825 Daniel O'Connell was in London agitating for Catholic emancipation. Griffin attended one of his addresses at a "Catholic meeting" in the Freemason's hall and was impressed by O'Connell's "uncompromising spirit, and wondered at the exemplary patience with which John Bull sat to hear himself charged with perfidy, etc., so roundly."[8] Attending the Clare elections in Ireland two years later on July 4, 1828, in which O'Connell was standing for a seat in the House, and doing so contrary to British law, Griffin noted his people's exemplary behavior. They appeared calm and resolute, and the young author knew at once that such conservatism would determine the fate of his nation. After witnessing O'Connell's defiance of British authority and his victory in the elections, he realized more than ever before that his people's moral behavior could be elevated through words, and not necessarily through the words of agitators alone.

IX   *The Critics*

On March 13, 1828, Scott made the following comments about the *Tales:* "The *Tales* are admirable. But they have one fault, that the crisis is in more cases than one protracted after a keen interest has been excited, to explain and to resume parts of the story which should have been told before. Scenes of mere amusement are often introduced betwixt the crisis of the plot and the final catastrophe. That is impolitic. But the scenes and characters are traced by a firm, bold, and true pencil, and my very criticism shows that the catastrophe is interesting,— otherwise who would care for its being interrupted?'"[9] Griffin's haste accounted for the structural fault Scott noted, but he was to correct this error in his new book without ever diminishing the pace at which he wrote.

The *Tales* were praised considerably by the critics, but the slight criticism he did receive, very similar to the constructive criticism of Scott, affected him so deeply that a year elapsed before he was able to settle upon his next story. *The Collegians*, once begun, however, was to create a passion in him so devastatingly alarming to his own spiritual peace that after its completion and reception by an enthusiastic public he was never again able to approach the subject of human passions in his writing.

X   The Collegians

Frequent visits to London accompanied the writing of the first half of *The Collegians*, for Griffin was always fretful about what public taste was demanding and how critics were responding to the plethora of new material reaching the market. Daniel, who had joined Gerald, witnessed the effort that went into the second half of the novel: "His imagination was so deeply impressed with the interest of every scene, that it gave to the whole theme the harmony and unity of a recollected truth rather than a creation, and the different characters were made to act and speak with a consistency and eloquence that showed how intimately he felt the situation they were placed in. On these occasions his old passion for the drama seemed to take the lead, and he framed every passage that was at all of a dramatic character with a view to the effect it would have in performance."[10] Yet he knew that the passion and art with which he completed his story far outweighed its didactic content. The fact that he had written a highly moral story was unimportant. The passion in his own breast which had helped to create *The Collegians* became anathema, and he resolved to atone for it in writing as soon as possible.

The Christian Physiologist was a part of this atonement. This strange collection of short tales was intended to teach the young how to govern the use of their senses. Daniel claimed it was very popular and obviously Gerald's future superiors in the society of Christian

Brothers thought so, for they wanted him to devote most of his time to
writing such pious literature. *The Christian Physiologist*, however,
was not a work of art, and Griffin must have known that its value in
terms of turning hearts to God was doubtful. He never wrote anything
like it again.

Still anxious to move ahead to new writing devoid of any taint of
passion, Gerald began research on the subject of the Viking invasion of
Ireland in the ninth century. His sole purpose was to acquaint his people with their ancient heritage, a patriotic and timely motive for an
Irish novelist in 1829 to adopt. So copious was his material for this
novel, *The Invasion*, that he had to delay its publication until 1832,
bringing out in 1830 a third series of the *Tales of the Munster Festivals*, which contained two novelettes, "The Rivals" and "Tracy's
Ambition." These two works, apparently started some time before he
began work on *The Collegians* and completed now to satisfy publisher
and readers, bore in greater measure the same promising qualities of
fine dramatic scenes and deep characterizations which the first series
had possessed. However, *The Invasion* proved to be a clear indication
to Griffin's public that history had, for some reason, eclipsed romance.
His readers were awash in "foreign" terms. Gaelic and Norse termi-
nology complicated narration and dialogue as two-dimensional characters traversed undefined landscape from Ireland to Sweden in the
ninth century.

On March 16, 1829, in the midst of his research for *The Invasion* at
the Dublin Library, Gerald wrote to William in a deeply religious tone
which also set forth his old fears and doubts, his superstitions and self-
recriminations, hardly natural for a young writer who was fast becoming a celebrity but characteristic of Griffin who was attempting to
withdraw more into the privacy of his Pallas Kenry home. He wrote,
in his private voice.

How I wish that I had enough of constancy and of generous resignation, as
well as of innocence, to cherish a perfectly quiet mind on this subject—to
say, "This project that I am forming is at least a harmless one, and may be a
useful one, if the Almighty suffer me to complete it; it will add to my own
enjoyment, and perhaps be of service to many around me; and if, on the
contrary, I should be interrupted in the course of it, why, it is still well that
I should be called away while I am harmlessly, and perhaps usefully occupied—as much so at least as circumstances will enable me to be." This is a
state of mind which I often contemplate with a longing eye, but my nature
is far from being equal to it. I have far too worldly a heart to observe the
proper distinction, to keep a just equilibrium, between a too keen interest in

my occupations, and an equally mischievous despondency and gloom. What terrifies me often, when I am inclined to let my heart expand a little on prospects of fortune, reputation, &c., &c., is the remembrance of the manner in which my last illness first came on. It was at the time when something like success—like hope, at least, began to draw upon me, and when I first began to convince myself that there was something like reason in my ambition. It then came all on a sudden, and like the shock of an earthquake; it was, in fact, death in everything but the one circumstance—that I did not die. Now, as my health improves, and the world begins to wind itself about my heart again, I am sometimes startled by the reflection, that as that sickness came then, death *will* come hereafter just as suddenly and unexpectedly. When I think of this at intervals, I shake my head, and wish I was a better Catholic.[11]

Such somber thoughts were soon forgotten, however, when Gerald made his entrance into the midst of Dublin's social and literary circles, quite by accident he said, as the result of stopping his work at the library to have tea with the surgeon-general, Sir Philip Crampton. His "far too worldly heart" swelled to the excitement of the adulation that Sir Philip and his friends bestowed upon him. Griffin wrote, in his public voice, to William on April 11, 1829, about his reception at Sir Philip's: "He liked my works so much that I dote on him already, as I do upon everybody that is not ashamed to praise me. And what affords me still greater, more heartfelt, and I hope not unworthy pride is, that Maria Edgeworth, who is intimate with the family, reads them with pleasure and speaks of them with approbation."[12] This enthusiasm was readily understood by William who felt that Gerald's high moral purpose in writing was merely eclipsed for the time in reaction to applause of which, previously and secretly, he had only dreamed. Now the dream was real, and in the same letter he wrote that only a lack of funds prevented his remaining another month among Dublin's first society: they were, after all, the only people to please in writing and actually the "only rank in which I could ever feel at home." But then, the second thought, with a dialogue: "Why was I not born to a fortune? If you were, says a little voice, you would never have known the Irish peasantry—you would never have written the Collegians—nobody would care a fig for you."

For the most part, the tone of this letter is touched with shades of jubilation, confidence, snobbery, and aspiration. However, far more often the presence of company, be they poets like Tom Moore or friends like John Banim, caused him pain and anxiety, the product of painful self-consciousness. As part of a reconciliatory letter sent to Banim on October 19, 1827, for example, Griffin confessed: "I never

entered your house without reluctance, even when you were most
warm and kind; excuse me if I could not do so when you seemed to
wear an altered face."[13] (So intense were Griffin's own feelings about
himself that he never considered that his friend might be in pain too.
Banim's facial expressions changed quite often during this early development of a paralysis that was eventually to take his life.) When Griffin was visiting Tom Moore, the poet actually caused an evening's company to become excessively animated to provoke Gerald into
conversation.[14] However, when he was invited to Mrs. James Fisher's
home near Limerick as the celebrated author of *The Collegians,* a
remarkable change took place in the man who cherished his privacy.

XI   *Gerald and Lydia*

Gerald was delighted with James and Lydia Fisher. They seemed to
combine, with such felicity, the business and culture of the world and
the care and Christian education of their children that Gerald was
immediately drawn to them. Lydia was passionately devoted to literature and the two immediately began collaborating. Correspondence
between the two soon began to reflect the depth to which Gerald's feelings were descending:

L——— [Lydia], write me longer letters when you write again, and don't
write about coming or going anywhere, but put the whole of Lydia's mind
and a piece of Lydia's heart upon the paper, and it will be to me as welcome
as the summer; and don't talk about forgetting, for if that began on either
side I promise you it will be on yours. To me such a friendship as I promise
myself yours will be, is a rare blessing, such as a poor author wants to console
him for a great deal of chagrin and disappointment; to keep his heart sweet
amid its struggles with an ugly world.[15]

Not since Ellen Griffin had sailed to America nearly a decade earlier
had Gerald known such feelings of security and tenderness as those he
was experiencing with Lydia Fisher. With James, Gerald was charming and revealing. In an undated letter he wrote: "My dear James,—I
am sorry I cannot be with you on Sunday. . . . I could say something
very edifying about the uncertainty of human affairs, but I never
preach except in print, and even then (Heaven forgive me!) only when
I think I am going to die."[16]

The Fishers and Gerald spent two weeks at the Irish lakes during the summer of 1829 traveling from Killarney to Kenmare, Glengarriff and Bantry; climbing mountains and boating; riding in jaunting carts through the slate-blue Gap of Dunloe in MacGillycuddy's Reeks. At the south end of the gap the trio enjoyed the beauty of the Upper Lake of the Lakes of Killarney to the southeast and Cummeenduff Glen to the southwest. But most enthralling for Lydia and Gerald were the wilds of Glengarriff which Gerald celebrated as the home of his idealized lovers Elim and Eithne in *The Invasion*.

Lydia remembered a trip to the wilds of County Kerry together one beautiful summer and wrote about it five years after his death. In a letter to a friend, she praises the beauties of Killarney, where she was then touring, when she remembers the presence of Gerald:

Yet, dearest S.———, the impressions made on the soul can only be portrayed by those who have experienced them, for
"He best can paint them who has felt the most" and those you shall have, for it is those you prize. Judge, then, if my happiness in gazing on those well-remembered scenes with those so dear to me, was not blended with a sorrowful recollection of the beloved friend, now no more, who was one of my companions when first their magnificence opened upon my enchanted eyes! So that, when the majestic Toomies with their waving woods, and the vast range at either side rose before me my eyes filled and my heart swelled with the memory of the past. The solemn panorama sunk into my soul which was impressed less by admiration than by sorrow! However, I strove to conquer my sadness, and to enter into the fresh young feeling of those now with me, who felt an intense and gay delight, such as belong to youth and innocence.[17]

Gerald's presence was felt even more intensely by Lydia in her next letter to the same friend about beautiful Glengarriff, forty-three miles to the south of Killarney:

I feel that no language can convey the slightest idea of the beauty of Glengarriff, which though thus called "the rough Glen," is adorned with the most soothing and tender loveliness. Here shut out from the rest of the world, one might contented live, contented die! My heart retains the impression most vividly . . . Glengarriff is retired and romantic; you feel that you would like to roam by that rushing river, and through those untrimmed groves, at any hour of the day, alone or accompanied, equally happy! . . . I have been here twice, and each time I have wished it were my home.[18]

Prompting the words of these letters might have been some lines Gerald wrote, "To Lydia":

VII
Oh, friend of my heart! if that doom should fall on me,
    And thou shouldst live on to remember my love,
Come oft to my tomb when the turf lies upon
    And list to the even wind mourning above.

VIII
Lie down by that bank, where the river is creeping
    All fearfully under the still autumn tree,
When each leaf in the sunset is silently weeping,
    And sigh for departed days, thinking of me.

IX
By the smiles ye have looked—by the words ye have spoken
    (Affection's own music, that heal as they fall)—
By the balm ye have poured on a spirit half broken,
    And, oh! by the pain ye gave—sweeter than all.

XII
And, oh! in that moment when over him sighing,
    Forgive, if his failings should flash on thy brain;
Remember, the heart that beneath thee is lying,
    Can never awake to offend thee again.

XIII
And say, while ye pause on each sweet recollection,
    "Let love like mine own on his spirit attend:
For to me his heart turned with a poet's affection,
    Just less than a lover, and more than a friend."[19]

"The pain ye gave" was too intense for such a moral man to bear. During this interval Lydia and Gerald's attraction for each other grew to love, but Gerald checked the situation by a sudden withdrawal from the Fisher's company and a return to work. From the evidence of Daniel's biography we can only speculate about Griffin's feelings during the years following that summer, when he saw less of Lydia Fisher but apparently still saw her. Daniel Griffin gives no indication that Griffin was avoiding Lydia, nor that he was continuing to experience deep satisfaction with the relationship. The letters dealing with this time indicate only that he was busy writing his books but was able to find some time to visit the Fishers.

One reaction to personal loss and failure may be increased religious scrupulosity, especially for someone like Griffin who had been moving steadily toward a higher moral purpose in his life. In a letter Ethel Mannin supplies, Griffin shows the same attitude toward the Fishers that he once showed Banim when they also were estranged. Mannin quotes and comments:

"Although I do not think it my duty to speak freely with you (without your express desire) of the principles on which I have acted, yet the intimacy which subsisted between us last year, and the sincere friendship which I retain for you and for every member of your family, render it, I believe necessary that I should offer some explanation." He goes on to explain that his time "cannot be allotted as formerly," consistent with his other obligations; that without the "slightest diminution of regard for you and all who are dear to you" he feels he must nevertheless live in retirement, and that in doing so he does right, acting on "the wisest principles for the regulation of my own mind."[20]

Mannin includes several other examples of what she terms "this excess of puritanism" which led ultimately to his vows of chastity, obedience, and poverty. But what she fails to note is that a bitterness began to grow in his heart, and as his private voice was raised increasingly to God his public voice condemned all that he had done. S. C. Hall wrote: "In 1836, when I saw him at Limerick, he had determined upon joining some religious fraternity. He had obtained and nourished an idea that his novels were sins, of which he ought to repent; and that poetry was an offering at the feet of Satan, instead of grateful incense to the God of Mercy and of Love."[21]

The day after Gerald was accepted into the order of the Christian Brothers, he wrote to William in a tone of regret and self-reproach which obviously flowed from his past relations with the Fishers:

I am grateful for the interest you all feel about me, dear William—I continue, thank God, better than I ever felt for so long a time together in my life— indeed if I could forget the past and become indifferent to what some particular friends may think of particular passages in it, I would be as happy as I could be in this world—these little recollections and the thought of these friends and of what they have thought or may still think and feel about me and my doings occasionally give me pain enough—however all in God's good time—His Holy Name be ever praised and blessed. The name I took in religion is Joseph. I had many good reasons for taking it any one of which if acted on for the rest of my days would be sufficient to make a saint—tisn't for want of reasons that people ever fail in becoming so.[22]

Romantic and tragic like Hardress Cregan, the hero of his only
"romance," *The Collegians*, Griffin imposed upon himself the same
fate his creation met: exile and death. Gerald died at the Cork monastery of typhus fever at 7:00 A.M., on Friday, June 12, 1840. He was
not alone. Daniel was at his side.

XII   *Griffin's Fiction: A Mandate from History*

Less than a generation after the Act of Union of 1800 Griffin began
to make his way in an English world of letters. He wanted to write
classical drama for the English stage but instead was forced to turn to
fiction and the subject of his Munster community. He possessed a profound knowledge of the Munster peasant who, during the eighteenth
century, suffered persecution under the Penal Laws. When Griffin
began writing about peasant life in his community, he did so with the
conviction that history must teach a lesson to the present generation
and not just satisfy the curious reader. He applied his talents to the
creation of accounts of conflicts among those men whose deeds composed the history of the Penal times of the eighteenth century down to
famines just preceding the year of Catholic emancipation, 1829. Griffin's fiction, therefore, is better appreciated in the light of the major
events in Ireland's history from the time of total conquest beginning in
the reign of Elizabeth I.

When a people are deprived of their natural rights, they tend to
think of their past, present, and future strictly in moral terms. From
the community squabble to the grand scale of national agitation such
a people will be combating essentially those forces denying them entry
into the civilized world where law means justice. The poet among
them—such as Gerald Griffin—will speak for his people as they stand
deprived of freedom and justice, and in the case of the Irish peasant,
of an identity that has sought "to win through to deliverance from an
organized system of tyranny and deliberate degradation which could
scarcely be paralleled in any other country."[23]

Ireland's history from the time of the Norman Conquest to the present explains the way of such Irish poets and writers as Griffin whose
art grew within the shadow of English domination. However, Griffin
was most particular, for in his work he sought a revitalization of the
creed that could turn minds to charity in daily living. In his writing he
emphasized spiritual well-being over temporal, but, at the same time,
he realized that a people deprived of their land tend quite naturally to
feel less than human. A champion of Catholics' rights, Edmund Burke

"argued that religion is the basis of civil society, which, in turn, is made for the advantage of man."[24] However, Griffin's themes evolved from the complex nature of a society whose issues of religion, politics, and race were hopelessly snarled. The measure of his success as a moralist and an artist is determined to a great extent by his faithful representation of this society and the history that shaped it.

CHAPTER 2

Penal Ireland

The Eighteenth Century

THE Norman Conquest of England in 1066 deepened Ireland's isolation from Europe. After the death of Brian Boru (in 1014), Ireland once again experienced political disunity but still maintained her ancient Gaelic Brehon law, "a certain rule of right unwritten, but delivered by tradition from one to another, in which often there appeareth great show of equity in determining the right between party and party,"[1] a law, stressing among many other things, communal ownership of land. Foreign rule of Ireland began in 1169 when Henry II's vassal, the earl of Pembroke, landed with a small army on the pretext of purging the Irish of their pagan ways. With this establishment, the old Brehon law was swept away, Norman castles appeared in the countryside, feudal ownership of the land that was actually under Anglo-Norman power followed, a government was set up in Dublin, and the liberties under the Magna Carta were extended in 1215 to Anglo-Norman Ireland. James Anthony Froude felt that: "Had the Irish been regarded from the outset as a conquered people whom a stronger neighbor had forced, for its own convenience, into reluctant submission, Ireland would have escaped the worst of her calamities. Her clans would have been held in awe by an army; public order would have been preserved by a police: but her lands would have been left to their native owners; her customs and her laws might have been untouched, and her religion need not have been interfered with."[2] England's mistake was in regarding Ireland not as a foreign country but as a part of her empire.

Because Ireland was never completely conquered by the English but rather garrisoned in all four corners, she became divided: the Anglo-Norman feudal world of castle and town life bordered the old Celtic world deeply committed to tribal customs, feuds, and disunity. Only one half of Ireland was ever under Anglo-Norman control at any one time, and by the fifteenth century the British rule was restricted to the Pale, the area today comprising County Dublin. By the fifteenth century Anglo-Norman towns were enjoying brisk trade with Spain and France, there was a monastic school system in the Gaelic tradition, and religious and social changes were taking place even within this two-world structure. With the accession of the Tudors, however, despotism set in: membership, for example, in the Irish parliament, first established in 1297, was limited to the Anglo-Norman or rather the Anglo-Irish by this time. The effect of such restriction meant, of course, that representation in the parliament did not go beyond the Pale.

The Reformation brought intolerance and division. Elizabeth's seizure of vast tracts of land meant eviction and starvation for thousands of peasants, but it also meant an alliance between those Anglo-Normans who had become quite Irish in family and custom and the native Gael. Henry VIII, having declared himself king of Ireland, countered this trend with the creation of an Irish nobility. His attempts to obliterate ancient Gaelic identity included destruction of Irish monasteries and condemnation of the pope. Protestantism was established during the reign of Edward VI, and Mary Tudor began the plantation system by which thousands of acres of Irish land were turned over to English settlers. Elizabeth established the Protestant Episcopal Church of Ireland, but Protestantism never took root, mainly because it was forced upon the peasant majority, but also because there was no middle class to support it. The outstanding effect of this Reformation upon the Irish people was that it added a religious factor to the already existing political one separating the two islands.

As a result of the Rebellion of 1641 in which the Irish Catholic clergy led a strike for religious freedom, Cromwell landed in force and within nine months killed six thousand persons and sent thirty-four thousand Irish soldiers into exile. More of a curse than Cromwell's work of putting down rebels was the loss of 750,000 victims to disease and starvation between 1641 and 1652. The Munster confiscation had been over one half million acres; added to this total were the Ulster and Cromwellian plantations comprising ten million acres. Thus a new landlord class evolved and held power for the next 250 years, but only through British force, which was ultimately to unite Gaelic Ireland and Protestant Ireland in a cause for political, economic, and religious freedom during the latter half of the eighteenth century.

Thus did a disenfranchised and landless people endure the endless strife, rebellion, and war which attended English rule in Ireland. How-

ever, by the beginning of the eighteenth century when nineteen-twen-
tieths of Ireland's land had been confiscated,[3] a feeling of national identity was beginning to take shape in the minds of many Irishmen and
a strategy for the duration of the English occupation was being
evolved. England's troubles abroad were Ireland's opportunities to
strike at home for her own good.

The eighteenth century, for the Catholic majority of Ireland, began
with the effects of James II's defeat at the hands of his son-in-law,
William III, in the Battle of the Boyne in 1690, which completed the
English conquest of Ireland. The Irish lost their lands, their religion,
and their civil rights. Protestant settlers became masters and native
Gaels, their slaves. The situation which evolved in the last few decades
of the century, however, proved startling for the Crown. David H.
Greene explains it:

It is one of the ironies of Irish history that the descendants of those Elizabe-
than, Stuart, Cromwellian and Williamite settlers who had resisted absorption
by the native Irish, now began to resist domination by the crown. No longer
in fact English but Anglo-Irish, they had begun to erect the big houses,
develop a distinctive culture of their own and build up industries which
placed them into direct competition with England. It was no longer the
impoverished and disfranchised Celts who provided rich pickings for the
royal treasury but the landowning Anglo-Irish capitalists who were building
breweries, manufacturing silk, glass and pottery and establishing a linen and
a cotton industry.[4]

Toward the end of the eighteenth century many Catholics were beginning to emerge as prosperous businessmen because of the easing of the
Penal Laws; Gerald Griffin's father was one of them. Maureen Wall
notes that since trade during the eighteenth century was held in contempt by gentlemen, "Catholics were permitted to control a large
share in the trade of the country. It was a lowly occupation, and it was
natural that they should be engaged in it; and since the law did not
permit them to buy land, they persevered in it until some of them
became quite wealthy."[5] The fact that they kept this wealth hidden
enabled them to become wealthy in spite of the Penal Laws leveled
against them at the beginning of the century.

The Anglo-Irish Parliament during Queen Anne's reign enacted the
Penal Laws to annihilate the Irish people. Under them no Irish Catholic could inherit land, buy it, or receive it as a gift from a Protestant.
Leases were limited to thirty-one years and profits held to one third of
the rent. An Irish Catholic could not vote, practice law, hold any civil

office, or serve in the British army or navy. W. E. H. Lecky, while noting the prostration of the Catholic peasantry under the Penal Laws, comments that Protestants were also weakened by an English parliament bent on the destruction of any Irish industry which could compete with England's.[6] Two points of grave significance pertaining to religion and land are also made by Lecky: although Catholicism was practiced freely some thirty years following the initial legislation of the Penal Laws, "the effect of those laws was to deprive law in Ireland of all moral sanction by bringing it into direct conflict with religion. The laws against property . . . were in a great degree automatic and they worked with terrible effect. One of the most serious effects was that nearly all Catholics of ability and energy abandoned either their country or their faith."[7] This situation left the Catholic majority without a leader from their own ranks for over one hundred years during which agrarian guerrilla warfare ranged to open rebellion in 1798. There seems little irony in the fact that support for the rights of Irish Catholics was to come during the eighteenth century mainly from Protestant leaders like Henry Grattan and Edmund Burke. Before their work for the relief of four-fifths of the population was felt, however, the Protestant Ascendancy sought supremacy and dominion over Catholic Ireland through their exclusive control of the Dublin Parliament and by the support given to them by the Episcopal Church of Ireland, which was supported by tithes extracted from destitute peasants. Burke termed the Anglo-Irish Protestant Ascendancy masters over the hordes of Irish Catholic peasants with the sole intent of making the wealth of Ireland their own.[8] As a member of the Ascendancy, Grattan worked against this purpose of which Burke spoke: his conservatism envisaged a Catholic membership within the Anglo-Irish Protestant Ascendancy.

The tyranny of the British Parliament in matters Anglo-Irish resulted in the ruin of the Irish woolen industry and the disintegration of Irish agriculture. The Cromwellian and Williamite wars had brought a great deal of land into disuse. The conversion of vast tracts to pasture for a quick return left thousands on the road to beg and starve. Those peasants who did manage to hold onto a patch of land came to depend upon a single crop, potatoes, so that when a crop failed, as in 1729 and 1740, hundreds of thousands died of starvation: "The potato . . . was a poor thing upon which to erect a society. The very ease with which it was grown helped to breed that improvident and devil-may-care attitude characteristic of Irish society during the 'gap in the famines,' between 1741 and 1822."[9] Aggravating the peasant farmer's miserable situation of having too little land to cultivate for bare subsistence were the exorbitant tithes and rents which resulted in sporadic warfare throughout the eighteenth century.

The practice of rack-renting forced the peasant to support a series of middlemen who handled an absentee lord's holdings in Ireland while the latter spent lavishly in London or on the Continent, always demanding more funds to be sent his way.[10] Swift noted that the practice went as far back as the Reformation, having been started by the powerful land-holding Episcopal hierarchy.[11]

By the middle of the century, the peasants began to move for independence. They banded together throughout the island and waged agrarian war as, for example, did the "Whiteboys" in Munster or the "Oakboys" in Ulster. The landlord was their prey and they attacked him, at times mercilessly. Weakened by the American war, Britain began to lose control over Ireland, and when one hundred thousand Irish Volunteers, armed supposedly for the event of a French invasion, demanded that the Dublin Parliament legislate for Ireland without interference from Westminster, they were successful for the moment. Grattan, who stood in front of the Volunteers but did not completely sanction their show of force, had this to say to his "nation" in the moment of triumph: "You, with difficulties innumerable, with dangers not a few, have done what your ancestors wished, but could not accomplish, and what your posterity may preserve, but will never equal: you have moulded the jarring elements of your country into a nation."[12] Rhetoric alone could never win for Grattan what he so earnestly desired. He "got his people their chance, and they were not fit to take it; they were, in fact, not yet a people. . . ."[13] The Irish Parliament was unable to establish a responsible government, and Grattan's movement to realize supremacy for the Ascendancy and greater equality for the Catholic gentry ended in dissention among the leaders within the movement and finally in the Act of Union in 1800. By the middle of the century, however, Catholics were enjoying greater religious freedom under a continuing relaxation of the Penal Laws.

The French Revolution had been initially a call to all mankind for regeneration, for reframing social and political order. But in the north of Ireland among Protestant dissenters a feeling of republicanism had been growing, particularly in view of the struggle of the American colonists. England's maltreatment of northern industries had driven many Scots-Irish to the American colonies, and those that remained were very susceptible to the overtures of Theobold Wolf Tone and his United Irishmen, formed as a consequence of revolutionary principles in Ireland and dissatisfaction with Grattan's undemocratic parliament.

Grattan and the Volunteers had failed, but what remained were the same economic problems crushing the hopes of northern Presbyterians and southern Catholics. Tone had attacked Grattan and his movement within the Irish Parliament. It was obvious to Prime Minister Pitt that open aggression from Tone's United Irishmen was imminent. Britain's having been at war with France had a great deal to do with the final decision; however, the suppression merely drove Tone underground, and the plot to overthrow the Irish government with France's aid was carried to its disastrous end for the rebels in the Rebellion of 1798.

The Catholic bishops, who had been enlisted by Pitt in his policies regarding imminent revolt, found themselves treated as never before by the British government. Their denunciation of the principles of the French Revolution followed by their condemnation of Tone's movement earned for them the status of trusted allies and a yearly grant of nine thousand pounds to support their seminary, founded at Maynooth in 1795. The British government was convinced that a priesthood hostile to the tenets of the French Revolution was a sound investment.[14] Such a harmonious arrangement between the British government and the Catholic hierarchy was in contrast to the horrendous Catholic and Presbyterian clashes in the north, the effects of which are still felt in Northern Ireland today. Catholic peasants in their zeal to acquire land began to pay higher rents than the Presbyterians were willing to do, thus forcing the latter off the land. After a battle between them in 1795 in which the Catholics were defeated, the Grand Orange Lodge of Ulster was founded and all that the United Irishmen had ever stood for in terms of religious toleration came to an end.

The United Irishmen, believing themselves strong in three-quarters of the island and ignoring all criticism emanating from the Catholic bishops, awaited Tone's landing with French troops, an event twice prevented by adverse weather conditions. Tired of waiting for French aid, the peasants rebelled on May 23, 1798, a date previously set by the United Irishmen. The insurrection took place mainly in County Wexford and defeat for the peasants came within eighteen days. The whole rebellion lasted but a month. Quite unexpectedly for Tone, in August of the same year, a French force of one thousand men landed in the west and initially put the British forces to flight. However, British reinforcements soon forced the French to surrender.

The Wexford Rebellion and the French landing convinced Pitt that the Irish Parliament must end and home rule begin; consequently, the Parliament was bribed by the British government and the Act of Union effected in 1800, with Ireland receiving one hundred seats in the British House of Commons and thirty-two seats in the House of Lords. The Anglo-Irish Ascendancy came to an end while the Irish Catholic peers and the Catholic bishops vainly awaited the emancipation promised to them by Pitt. Unfortunately, George III would not consent to such a step, and the Catholic majority were forced to wait nearly three decades for the work of the Liberator, Daniel O'Connell.

In 1803, the year in which Gerald Griffin was born, another attempt at rebellion was tried. Robert Emmet, an ardent nationalist, led fifty slum-dwellers of Dublin against the British Empire. His act would surely have remained as it had begun, a ludicrous venture, but his eloquence, dignity, and courage in the face of his merciless captors won for Ireland another name for freedom. From the dock and before an impatient judge, Emmet spoke: "I have but one request to ask at my departure from this world; it is the charity of its silence. Let no man write my epitaph; for as no man who knows my motives dare now vindicate them. Let them rest in oblivion and my tomb remain uninscribed, until other times and other men can do justice to my character. When my country takes her place among the nations of the earth, then, and not till then, let my epitaph be written."[15] Daniel O'Connell shaped an entire national front in opposition to British rule, but his methods differed completely from those suggested in the simple sacrifice of a single life.

Nearly sixty coercion acts were passed by the British government to insure that Ireland would not rise again. No government could foresee, however, the events that were to unfold as a result of O'Connell's vows to win emancipation and gain repeal of home rule. Having organized the peasants with the help of the priests of Ireland, O'Connell was able to win emancipation for Catholics who had begun to experience an atmosphere of toleration as far back as the middle of the eighteenth century. Repeal of union he failed to obtain: at the time, England could hardly be expected to forget the role Ireland could play in a possible invasion of British shores.

O'Connell's lack of leadership was felt in his failure to cope successfully with the agrarian problem still ravaging Ireland.[16] Moreover, the tithe was still in effect, causing many peasants to rebel and suffer loss of property. After five years of open violence, from 1833 to 1838, a compromise was reached whereby a twenty-five percent reduction in tithes was granted to the Catholic, with the landlord now levied with an additional charge. However, this solution failed since the landlord merely raised his tenants' rents to reimburse himself.

The Education Act of 1831 reflects shortsightedness on O'Connell's part in addition to failure to tend successfully to agrarian and tithe reform. The Act called for a public elementary school system in which only English was to be spoken and only English history and literature were to be taught. Ireland's cultural legacy thus would be driven from the minds of peasants—or so that British government hoped.

By 1840 O'Connell knew that the British Parliament would never repeal the union. His tactics of the past, mainly dependent upon the voice of a united peasant front, led to his founding the Repeal Association and organizing huge "monster meetings" in attempts at intimidating the British once more. In 1843, at the climax of his campaign for repeal of union, a meeting was called for at Clontarf. The British banned it and O'Connell, rather than see bloodshed, complied. Soon after he spent one year in prison, having remembered, no doubt, how he once called for violence in the cause.

O'Connell brought the Irish Catholic peasant's mind into the modern world and out of the despair of eighteenth-century history. Under his leadership they acquired a sense of nationhood, identified by the faith of the Catholic Church. O'Connell was a figure whom Griffin applauded at the Clare election in 1828, a figure who was doing what no man before him had done for the people of Ireland: he was leading them to unity, to identity, and to purpose as Catholic free men who must hold their land. Regardless of how much O'Connell neglected agrarian reforms, failed to achieve repeal of union, and displayed passion and appetites unbecoming a leader of a Catholic nation, he restored a great measure of life and spirit to a people slated for extinction by the British government and the Anglo-Irish Ascendency a century or more before his coming.

Such government had been accompanied by confiscation, famine, overpopulation, expansion of pasturage, armies of unemployed laborers, backward agricultural practices, unfair British trade practices, rack-renting landlords, agrarian violence, tithes—all in opposition to the common meaning of Christian charity. Deprived of his land, the peasant tended to think of himself less as a member of any community, either spiritual or temporal, and more as an outlaw. Never a part of the establishment, the peasant ruled himself through base instincts and always with a sense of sympathy for his kind. This majority—of landless and long-suffering peasants—was Griffin's subject to a large extent. He recorded their character and their history. When he saw that he would have to continue to create the passions of characters like Hardress Cregan in his own breast before he was able to set them down on paper, he finally abandoned art.

CHAPTER 3

Years of Conversion

*G*ISIPPUS and *Holland-tide* are Griffin's first works and as such manifest the earliest signs of his talent for writing highly didactic literature. More than this, however, they show that the effects of his conversion from classic drama to prose fiction meant the coming of his art for one who knew the nature of his people and found he was able to dramatize it in prose. His themes now entered all that was a part of him: the land, the people, and their history. His genius flourished with such elements. When he forgot them in his last two novels, *The Invasion* (1832) and *The Duke of Monmouth* (1836), the deadening effect of his fanatic religiosity was compounded by material for which he had no talent.

I Gisippus

Gisippus was written on scraps of paper in London coffeehouses over a period of several months and later transcribed. Griffin did no research. He had his education in the Latin classics, his intimacy with Shakespeare, and his experience with the Limerick Thespians from which to draw. However, in the writing, *Gisippus* became an autobiographical piece in the creation of the main characters, Gisippus and Fulvius.

II *Summary and Analysis of* Gisippus

Gisippus demonstrates the causes and remedies for the dissolution and reestablishment of a friendship between two young noblemen, Gisippus of Athens and Fulvius of Rome. The two have just completed their education at the Lyceum, and Gisippus is about to marry a resigned Sophronia when Fulvius discovers his friend's betrothed is none other than the woman he has been in love with for three years but who he thinks has spurned him for another. Although Gisippus is deeply in love with Sophronia, and incidentally needs her wealth to stave off his creditors, he nevertheless gives her to his friend as he struggles vainly to experience the "virtue" of sacrifice. His creditors lay hold of him, and when Fulvius and Sophronia set off for Rome, fame, and wealth, Gisippus is sold into slavery. Finally, the two collegians are reunited in Rome at a time when Fulvius, now a Roman praetor, has just arrived from a successful expedition against the Armenians. Gisippus is so maddened by Fulvius' seeming callousness that he attempts suicide by assuming responsibility for a murder he did not commit. At the moment he is to die, Fulvius intervenes and shortly restores their friendship.

Griffin wrote to William about his main characters on May 18, 1824: "Gisippus I have made a fellow of exquisite susceptibility, almost touching on weakness; a hero in soul, but plagued with an excessive nervousness of feeling, which induces him to almost anticipate unkindness, and of course drives him frantic, when he finds it great and real— at least apparently so. Fulvius is a sincere fellow, but an enthusiast for renown, and made insolent by success."[1] Wittingly or otherwise, both characters are drawn from the "soul" of their author who crammed most of the themes about which he was to write for the next fourteen years into this play: passion, friendship, marriage, education, love, virtue, ambition, honor, duty to a supreme being, the dream, the pagan conscience, forgiving and forgetting, and redemption.

Passion drives the unreasoning couple, Fulvius and Sophronia, into each other's arms. They choose marriage on the basis of physical attraction. Fulvius' insensitivity to the sacrifice his friend is making also is an indication of the extent to which his education has not prepared him for life. For Fulvius, love and lust are indistinguishable. Moreover, once ambition takes hold of the Roman, he begins to abuse all who have served him well, particularly his wife. The remorse he later feels is left to an awkward admission that his conscience, all the while he strives for fame, power, and wealth, preys heavily upon him. A pagan conscience informs Gisippus that in his sacrifice for the happiness of a friend he would experience the joy of a more virtuous existence. This is not to be. Others in the play, most notably Medon, Sophronia's brother, show some signs of spiritual awakening toward the end when the lesson of Fulvius and Gisippus is placed clearly before their eyes.

Throughout his trials, Gisippus maintains his honor and does not rebuke his old friend, yet his honor and virtue, neither mitigating pain nor bringing peace to his troubled mind, seem little consolation for his suffering. In chains and about to be executed, Gisippus cries out:

> Invisible Ruler! should man meet thy trials
> With silent and lethargic sufferance,
> Or lift his hands and ask heaven for a reason?
> Our hearts must speak—the sting, the whip is on them;
> We rush in madness forth to tear away
> The veil that blinds us to the cause. In vain!
> The hand of that Eternal Providence
> Still holds it there, unmoved, impenetrable;
> We can but pause, and turn away again
> To mourn—to wonder—and endure.[2]

The novels that Griffin later wrote answer this anguished cry with the Christian stoicism of the Catholic faith.

The last act quickly focuses upon six themes which are to become prominent in Griffin's future writing. Here, the dream makes its appearance as a theme in four lines, spoken by Gisippus as he is about to meet Sophronia for the first time since last he saw her in Athens:

> My dreams have been of this! My sleep has been
> Fear haunted, till this vision came to quiet it,
> And then my soul knew peace! O ye have been
> My memory's mighty visitant.[3]

Later, in prose, Griffin deepens the psychological significance of the dream, fusing it to other social and moral themes.

Fulvius is able to redeem himself with Gisippus because as an honorable and generous official of the state he has been good to his people. Sophronia's "reconciling influence" in the whole affair, her sway over Gisippus and Fulvius in the scene Banim thought so worthy of production, is owed, no doubt, to her appearance as one who has had little pleasure in her life since all three were together in Athens. Sophronia also provides an excellent example of the irony which is so prevalent in the play. She reasons like a student of the Lyceum in an attempt to cool Fulvius' ardor once he determines to take her from Gisippus. When, however, Gisippus releases her from her promise to wed him, she immediately forgets Gisippus' nobility and devotion to her in her haste to wed Fulvius.

The ideals of this young poet sponsored the highly improbable characters of Gisippus and Fulvius, later to become Hardress Cregan and

Kyrle Daly in *The Collegians*. For Griffin, it was not just the writer's convention of posing opposites. In writing about ambition and spirituality, pride and stoic honor, fame and anonymity, Griffin was writing about his agony: he was alone in a world seemingly hostile to both his principles and his art.

Inextricably a part of those truths closest to the heart and mind of the author are the social or public themes of family pride, social reform, justice, and class division. These themes are to make Griffin, together with Maria Edgeworth and John Banim, one of the first spokesmen for social reform in Ireland in the opening decades of the nineteenth century.

In *Gisippus*, Griffin dramatizes the ill effects of family pride. Medon, Sophronia's brother, orders the men of his house to destroy Gisippus for giving Sophronia to a Roman, thus depriving his family of the opportunity of becoming allied to one of the most prestigious families in Athens. He is soon compensated, however, when Fulvius takes him to Rome and shares the good fortunes which are suddenly descending upon him. Fame and wealth apparently do little to prevent his dealing honorably and justly with all the citizens of Rome who come under his sway. This fact is the single redeeming feature of Fulvius' life since last the two friends met.

One of Griffin's most effective devices for reversing the course of a story is his use of the theme of rendering justice through law. Gisippus, bloody sword in hand, is found standing over the body of his supposed victim. Justice eventually is done in the play as the author hoped some day it would be done in Ireland. It is clear that Griffin desires reform not only for the English stage but also for the English government whose coercive acts were oppressing Ireland at the time. The charge made against Gisippus by Medon and the people of Athens is that he has a rich friend in the Roman but allows himself to go to ruin. The political implication is that Ireland be damned for thinking England her friend while war, pestilence, and starvation crush the majority of Ireland's citizens.

III Gisippus *Performed*

The production of *Gisippus* took place on February 23, 1842. William Charles Macready was then the lessee of Drury Lane and set upon Gerald's original ambition in writing—raising the standard of the London stage. William Griffin sold the *Gisippus* manuscript, which Gerald had given to him the day he burned most of his other works, to

Macready for a handsome price, and the actor realized a profit from a very successful season. He acted in the title role, and so enthusiastic were the responses from audiences that season that one critic wrote: "That Macready will succeed in restoring the classical drama to the stage no one can doubt."[4]

Today *Gisippus* exists not as a work of art but as an indication of Griffin's potential. It is melodramatic and excessively sentimental; its characters are highly improbable and its themes far too many. However, in Griffin's themes and, at times, in his flashes of brilliant dialogue are the signs that this young Irishman could serve art and society. Criticism arriving thirteen years after the play's performance sees Griffin as a promising young playwright whose talent, unfortunately, "did not meet at once with fostering encouragement in the line to which it was at first so strangely turned."[5] John Banim was unable to get *Gisippus* played, but he did a great deal to foster his friend's talent for writing dramatic prose.

IV   Holland-tide

The success of Banim's *Tales of the O'Hara Family* prompted the author to invite Griffin to contribute. He refused the generous offer, but prompted by William, who surprised him with a visit in September, 1826, he began to write about his people and their neighborhood.

William wrote to Daniel concerning Gerald's initiation: "Most of the tales in *Holland-tide* were written in an inconceivably short space of time (not more than two or three months) before their publication, and entirely at my constant urging, and I can testify, from the difficulty I had in inducing him to make the effort at all, how very diffident and doubtful he was of success."[6] Doubt arose from the time factor. Gerald had his commitments to the journals to think of as well. However, the creative power and intensity of Banim's realism in the *O'Hara Tales* supported the conversion. Griffin was to follow his friend in "the very easy and natural drama that is carried through them [the *O'Hara Tales*] as well as in the excellent tact which he shows, in seizing on all the points of national character which are capable of effect."[7] Banim's intention in literature—"the formation of a good and affectionate feeling between England and Ireland"[8]—was consonant with Griffin's own and as such was adopted for *Holland-tide* and future work.

Holland-tide consists of seven tales of varying lengths, the longest and best of which is "The Aylmers of Bally-Aylmer." The story, Daniel wrote, "was almost the only tale in this series that had any pretension to a deep-wrought interest, and even upon this he did not appear to have spent any extraordinary pains.'"9 Daniel's observation seems quite accurate, and for this reason a critical analysis of the story may suffice in evaluating Griffin's first effort in the new genre. One other tale, approximately one-third the length of "The Aylmers," entitled "The Hand and Word," also deserves commentary because its relative success as a shorter piece suggests that Griffin profited greatly by such experimentation before moving on to full-length novels.

As a device for commencing his tales, Griffin gathers peasants at the hearth of a prosperous Kerry farmer on the evening of the holy feast of Holland-tide, All Soul's Day, for the purpose of having each tell his story after his own fashion—"something about wakes and weddings, and them things. . . . Or smugglers, or coiners, or fighting at fairs . . . or rebellion, or murthering of one sort or another."10 Griffin's own vivid recreation of hidden, Gaelic Ireland commences in the very opening of the book:

"HOLLAND-TIDE," "All-Hollands," "Hollands-Eve," and November-Eve, was once a merrier time in Ireland than it is at present, though even still its customary enjoyments are by no means neglected. Fortunately for "all the Saints," in whose honour the feast is celebrated, it occurs at a season of the year when the pressure of want is less sensibly felt than at most others, and, among a people who are, generally speaking, so easily satisfied as to the external comforts of life, that a comparative alleviation of suffering is hailed with as hearty a welcome as if it were a positive acquisition of happiness. The peasant sees, at this period at least, the assurance of present abundance around him. He beholds a vast extent of land all cultivated, and burdened with the treasured produce of the soil—gardens of stubble covered with shocks of wheat, oats, and barley, which look just as if they were intended to make bread for him and his neighbours; fields of potatoes, some in which the numberous earthen mounds, or *pits*, have been already raised; others, in which the nipping frost that is borne on the November blast has embrowned the stalks and withered the leaves upon their stem. The stroke of the flail and the clack of the water-mill are in his ear—the meadow land is green and fresh with its aftergrass—and the *haggart*, or hay yard, is stacked in to a labyrinth with hay and corn. He is satisfied with the appearance of things about him—he thinks he has no business asking himself whether any of these good things are destined for his use, or for that of a foreign mechanic—he never stops to anticipate in fancy, while he puts the spade for the first time into his own little half acre, and discloses the fair produce of his labour, how many calls from tithe-proctor, assessed tax-gatherer, landlord, priest, etc., may yet diminish his little store: he sees the potatoes; they are his and his pig's by right, and he and his pig are merry fellows while they last, and while they can produce a turfen fire, or the smoke of a fire, to warm the little cabin about them.[11]

The social disparity under the fleeting spell of holiday cheer immediately sets the tone for all that follows, and, beginning with "The Aylmers of Bally-Aylmer," Griffin's creative genius becomes apparent. Now he is dealing with a people he has "actually lived among ... sleeping at the farmers' houses, sitting at the fireside with the farmer and his family, talking freely to the servant boys and girls, hearing them tell stories, describe events, and drop out unconsciously their humour and wit. Of all these he took notes. He had a most intimate acquaintance with every part of the country where he lived. He spent days and nights wandering about exploring its beauties, conversing with the country people, and gathering every grey legend floating among the inhabitants" (*H*, 9).

V   *"The Aylmers of Bally-Aylmer": Summary and Analysis*

The story is set on the Atlantic coast of County Kerry, in and about the assize town of Tralee in approximately the year 1800 when Ireland was united to England through the Act of Union. This union meant the loss of all semblance of self-rule; one consequence was the imposition by the British government of numerous coercive measures which continued in force for the next sixty years. Hence, the themes of lawlessness and justice are prominent in the story of young William Aylmer and the "murder" of his father.

Will's journey from Dublin, where he has attended college, to the home of his guardian Cahill Fitzmaurice, comprises the opening movement of the story. Once he emerges from the adventure of his trip, the narrator introduces through flashback the sinister background of Fitzmaurice, who has been a smuggler and is now living quite comfortably upon his farm with his daughter Kate. When Will and Kate are reunited, the action moves swiftly ahead to the climax of Fitzmaurice's trial at the assizes in Tralee in which the "ghost" of the man Fitzmaurice is reputed to have murdered, Will's father Robert Aylmer, appears to give testimony. Two deft strokes of dramatic structuring, Will's journey home and his pursuit of justice in Tralee, uncover the lawlessness that was to be found in the mountains of Kerry and the social chaos which became apparent in the homes and town life of this locale around the year 1800. For men like Fitzmaurice and Robert Aylmer are magistrates of a law that the garrison represents. They are of the old establishment who have never accepted British dominance and who have learned to grow rich through smuggling.

A precise balancing of scenes is the principal feature in Griffin's "The Aylmers." The lawlessness in the Kerry hills which Will uncovers on his journey to the home of his benefactor Cahill Fitzmaurice is matched by the lawlessness in the old smuggler's history which Will also discovers in a very short time. William has been raised by old Cahill Fitzmaurice and never has heard a word directed against him as the murderer of William's father, Robert, Fitzmaurice's former partner in the old trade. Griffin displays his fine dramatic talent for dialogue, situation, and humor in the opening pages of the story in which Will seeks direction from the hostess of an inn on the Limerick-Kerry border:

> "The mountains! The Kerry hills! Alone by yourself, and at this time o'night! Now, hear to me, will you, sir, for it's a lonesome way you're taking, and them mountains is the place for all manner of evil doings from the living and from the dead. Take this little bottle of holy water, and shake a little of it upon your forehead when you step upon the heath. Walk on bold and straight before you, and if the dead might come upon you, which I hope no such thing will happen till you reach Tralee any way, you won't whistle: don't, for it is that calls 'em all about one if they do be there; you know who I mean, sir. If you chance to see or hear anything bad, you have only to hold these beads up over your head, and stoop under it, and, whatever it is, it must pass over the beads without doing you any harm. Moreover—"
>
> "Easy, easy, Mrs. Giltinaan, if you please. There is something of much more consequence to me than those fine instructions of yours. Don't mind telling me what I shall do in case I lose my way, until you have let me know first how I am to find it."
>
> "Oh, then, why shouldn't I, and welcome, Mr. Aylmer? Listen to me and I'll tell you, only be careful and don't slight *themselves* for all." (*H*, 11–12)

Mrs. Giltinaan's charming mixture of religious sentiment and superstition is in counterpoint to Will's own lack of awareness of what awaits him at journey's end. However, it is Will who will relieve two old men, Cahill Fitzmaurice and Robert Aylmer, of their self-imposed sentences of despair and exile.

As Will continues his journey the narrator entertains his readers with some disclosures about the collegian's parent. Both the moral and the story begin to unfold, society and artist collaborating to teach and entertain. Griffin's technique is to create thematic action uncovering the social, economic, and religious status quo of the neighborhood. The

moral, once it begins to emerge, is kept before the reader through continued excitement, songs, humor, and abundant dialogue. Society with
its ills is never condemned; all within come to learn the moral of the
lesson they have lived. Free will overcomes besetting sins. Griffin's
society is no Godwinian wasteland: his characters save themselves for
God's reward. And as thickly melodramatic as they sometimes become
in the process, for the most part they are strikingly attractive types and
quite entertaining.

The narrator now begins his history of Aylmer and Fitzmaurice.
Robert Aylmer has lived well on the proceeds from his smuggling until
he needs a sum which requires more risk than he was ever before
required to take. Such "broken gentlemen" have little else to do with
their wealth but to entertain one another, throwing their doors open to
their peasant followers as well. He and Cahill Fitzmaurice or Cahill-
cruv-dharug (Cahill-of-the-red-hand) undertake a dangerous affair
and, being successful, continue on to even more dangerous ones.
Returning from one on a Galway hooker in a gale, the two quarrel and
Cahill tosses Robert over the side. Supposedly he perishes. A jury subsequently acquits Cahill who adopts Aylmer's son, raises him along
with his own daughter Kate until the boy is ten, and then sends him
off to the "metropolis," Dublin. Will, now returning to the home of his
benefactor after an absence of nine years, has to cross the Kerry mountains, giving Griffin his first opportunity to introduce the landscape and
the people.

Between Will and the homes of his father and his benefactor, Bally-
Aylmer and Kilavariga, lie, "heath beyond heath, and bog after bog,
as far as his sight could reach in prospect, canopied over by a low dingy
and variable sky, and rendered still more dispiriting by the passing
gusts of wind which occasionally shrieked over the desolate expanse
with so wildering a cadence as almost to excuse the superstition of the
natives, that the fairies of the mountain ride in the blast; these formed
the prominent characteristics of the scene which lay before him" (H,
14). Fairies and superstition are two notes which build to such a
"shriek" in the story that when the "ghost" of Robert Aylmer appears
to his son, the young man's Dublin sophistication vanishes.

At present, however, Will is imperturbable, even when an old man
suddenly steps before him out of the black of a mountain trail warning
him not to travel the mountains at night and asking him to deliver a
letter to Bally-Aylmer. Will laughs, "'My head is filled with tales of the
Kerry mountains, and their marauders, and banathees, and phukas; but
for the one, I am provided with this amulet,' brandishing his beads,

'and here is a charm for the other,' elevating his stout black-thorn in a gay humor" (*H*, 17). Before Will leaves the old man, he catches a glimpse of his face and there is an instant feeling of recognition which quickly passes in the excitement of an encounter with thieves, a chase, and his arrival at Bally-Aylmer.

A storm develops as Will proceeds along the bog trail and when a cabin appears, he does not hesitate to enter: "Boloa irath! (Bless all here) he exclaimed as he bent forward over the half-door, willing to conciliate the good-will of the inmates by affecting a familiarity with their habits and language" (*H*, 20). An old woman, Vauria, with a short pipe in her mouth, returns the greeting as Will hangs his coat to dry by the turf fire and sets to devouring the mutton, potatoes, and oaten bread which the old woman places before him. Presently, two men arrive who ask the stranger if he speaks English. When Will replies that he does not, they proceed to reveal their identity as "a gang of the far-famed Kerry sheep-stealers" with an intimate knowledge of his father's death. Apparently the thieves, Lewy most prominently among them, have just returned from a raid on Cahill's flocks. One of them begins to tell about it:

"Lewy did a purty piece o' work this evening . . . Cahill-cruv-dharug's herdsman will be missen a ha' porth o' tar in the mornen. One of the prettiest creatures an the long walk, and fat, ready melt in our arms. Take it from me, Vauria, Cahill Fitzmaurice won't be a bit glad to be eased of her, tomorrow morning."

"Let him score it over against the blood of Robert Aylmer, then, and he'll be the gainer still, may be," muttered the old woman. "Pho! Pho! Easy. What nonsense you talk. Wasn't he cleared o' that be a judge an jury, in the face o' the whole country?—Pho!"

"I was aboord the boat that awful night, an I heard words spoken that oughtn't to pass a Christian's lips, except he was a Turk. But what's the use of being talking? There's as much time to come after as ever went before us, an they say blood will speak if it bursts the grave for it." (*H*, 22)

The old woman's words are both ironic and prophetic—ironic because Will is for the first time learning about his father's death and prophetic because his father will soon speak to him about the matter.

Moments after this exchange takes place Will finds an opportunity to burst from the cabin which very likely will mark the site of his grave if he remains. Chase is given by the gang with their hound "Caesar" but Will eludes them: "Blessed Saviour o' the airth!—O Lewy! the sthrame!—We're lost for ever! Come back here, Sayzer!—The

unnait'rcl, informing Dane! To come among us and make a fool of a
shoulder of as good mutton as was ever dhrov the wrong way off a
sheep-walk. . . ." (*H*, 29). Young Aylmer hurries on, making his way
now for Bally-Aylmer, rest, and a fresh suit of clothes before he
appears before Cahill and Kate in the morning.

With the cabin scene Griffin begins his commentary on the themes
of justice and law in Ireland. British law exists in the minds of British
magistrates, Anglo-Irish Protestants like Geoffrey Hasset in this story.
Cases which come before him or before British judges receive punishment under British law, which quite often remains incongruous to circumstances which exist in Ireland. Since the Irish peasant does not recognize the existence of British law, when he enters a courtroom he is
as evasive as his talents permit. Cahill is never convicted because no
witness like old Vauria testifies against him. He is, however, condemned by the community to live a friendless and empty life, for he
broke the law which really governs the consciences of these Kerry peasants, namely, their own law. Hence, Cahill is living on the spoils of his
old smuggling days, and Lewy has no compunctions about taking from
this outsider. If more retribution is to come, let it come from the grave,
as old Vauria says it may.

Bally-Aylmer is more than "one of those architectural testimonies to
the folly of our fathers, which are scattered rather abundantly over the
face of the green isle" (*H*, 30). It is a symbol of the injustice that befell
its country and a spiritual decay that perpetuates its ruin. Will enters
the ruin to discover his father's old servant Ally Culhane and her son
Sandy. Ally is a part of the ruin. She knew Robert Aylmer when he
first threw open his doors to entertain all who came to praise the daring
that had made it possible. Before her now stands Will Aylmer who has
been raised by Cahill of the red hand, the "murderer" of her master.
The resemblance he bears to his father shocks the old lady, as it is soon
to do Cahill. The narrator leaves Will to rest for his meeting with Cahill in the morning and turns to an interview which has begun about the
time of young Aylmer's arrival at Bally Aylmer.

Just as Ally is shocked by the sight of Will's resemblance to his
father, so Kate, in hearing for the first time the story of her father's
relationship with Aylmer upon the occasion of Will's expected arrival,
receives a similar jolt. As the interview progresses, the narrator speaks
privately to his reader about the old man:

Though he was a native of a country where more apologies are found for the
shedding of human blood than would, if universally admitted, greatly further

the interests of society, and although much of his life had passed amid scenes where homicide was familiar as the day-light, Cahill Fitzmaurice had, either from a natural quickness of feeling, or from the influence of that half-animal, half-chivalrous sense of moral honour which is so often made to supply the place of system, of principle, or of true religion in the minds of a neglected people, retained a tetchiness of spirit about what he was pleased to call his reputation, which would come with an ill grace enough from the lips of a smuggler of the present day. (*H*, 32–33)

What remains of "that half-animal, half-chivalrous sense of moral honour" that has guided Cahill in smuggling, what emerges from a "paroxysm of despair" following his realization that only a British court has acquitted him, is despair and the occasional recognition of his daughter's presence and beauty.

Kate listens to her father and is not repelled. She has lived with him all her life and has been educated by him. No trace of his "crime" seems evident in her appearance or behavior. The narrator ascribes to Kate's attention to her father an "unintended, undetected self-seeking . . . portion of the deep devotedness of love, with which the merry-hearted Kate abandoned herself in the full glow of youth, and with the fullest capability for the enjoyment of more congenial society to the silence, the solitude, and the gloom of her father's dark oaken parlour" (*H*, 36). This aspect of Kate may seem natural in anyone who lives outside the pale of Cahill Fitzmaurice, who stands untried and condemned before his community.

The past and the present are also part of the scene that follows Cahill's interview with his daughter. As Kate becomes enlightened about her father's past, Will likewise recognizes for the first time in his life the ruin that has been his home. This somber moment, however, is broken by an old foxhunting song Sandy Culhane begins to sing:

> "Good morrow, Fox".—"Good morrow, sir,"
>   "Pray what is that you're ating?"
> "A fine fat goose I stole from yuce;
> Pray, will you come and taste it? . . ."
> "But I promise you, you'll sorely rue
> That fine fat goose you're ating!" (*H*, 43)

Sandy, soon to become Will's follower, reminds the reader that Lewy and his followers have robbed Will's guardian and given the collegian cause to seek their punishment in a British court. Provincial Ireland, however, is not Dublin, as Will soon discovers when he opposes Lewy.

When Will appears before Ally and Sandy dressed in the only clothes he is able to find, his father's old sea togs, old Ally is amazed at the resemblance of father and son. Even more startling is the impression Cahill receives. Griffin compresses time in these two recognition scenes to intensify the action of the reunion of Cahill and Robert Aylmer in the final courtroom scene. Will now advances on Kilavarig with childhood memories exciting his hopes for a delightful encounter with Kate. She too is seeking great pleasure in their meeting again, but Griffin has prepared some initial disappointment which they have to overcome. Will sees none of the "exquisite combination of colour in the cheeks—no lilies and roses—no rubies—no diamonds"; he appears to her "a well-looking, clever young fellow, rather under the stature of masculine beauty, and with, to a prophetic eye, a promise of rotundity in his person" (H, 48–49). Griffin, in bringing them a step closer and giving each a second look, seems to be preparing his reader for interaction and conflict. Will muses:

—and yet the face itself was perfectly captivating. Her lips were thin, but eternally charged with an expression of arch gravity or undisguised pleasure which the restless heart supplied in such continual succession as totally to exclude all thought of considering their pretensions to mere maternal beauty. Her eye was gray and shrewd, in its moments of comparative inaction, but full of fire, of passion, of mirth, of thought, of feeling, or of *fun*, according as those varying emotions were stirred up within her bosom. The whole countenance fell into a character of intensity and animation, which gave the fairest promise in the world of evenness that might be expected from the mind and temper. (H, 48)

Kate considers Will:

His face was a good oval, indicative of strong intellect, but perhaps quite as much, or rather more so, of strong passion, his forehead round and resolute, his eyebrows so Melpomenish, that they would have given a moped and anxious air to his *masque* if they were not corrected by vigour and bustle of the eye beneath them: that was an article of the greatest advantage to the character of the whole face. There was no affectation about it and yet it was full of meaning, and had a frankness that was royal. His hair, rather black, and doubtful whether it should curl or no, was thrown back on all sides in a kind of floating way, an arrangement that savoured too much of technicality, when it is considered that he was a haunter of Parnassus. (H, 49)

Will and Kate seem quite prepared to continue their calm appraisal of each other, but when old Fitzmaurice makes his entrance and sees the image of Robert Aylmer, he nearly collapses: "May the great and merciful Lord of the universe forgive us all! Surely we are none of us without our weakness! William, do I deserve this of you?" (*H*, 50). He deserves punishment but not the kind to which he has been subjecting himself for so many years. His God's mercy means confession and repentance, but his pride has brought him to despair.

The following morning old Cahill appears in good spirits and with Kate welcomes the collegian home with a great deal of warmth and enthusiasm. In his jubilation at now being so happily restored with his guardian, Will gives an account of his meeting with the sheep-stealers and determines to take action with the magistrate, Mr. Geoffrey Hasset of Hassetville. Fitzmaurice is opposed to the action, but Will wants justice for his benefactor and sets out for Hassetville. The scene that follows presents an uncommon occurrence among the peasants, but one which they never fail to relish. It is the return of the absentee landlord, Geoffrey Hasset, and Griffin's theme of justice is delivered in the tumultuous reception the great man receives. The scene is charged with action, humor, pathos, and prophecy. The initial condescension of Hasset to their play is turned to dismay as his tenants swarm over his carriage, jeer and lecture him for his absence and neglect, and finally commandeer his carriage, dispersing the horses and propelling the vehicle to the gates of Hasset castle.

As this scene erupts, the outlaw peasants are poised in the hills surrounding Hassetville ready to make their entrance and to take part in the games and celebrations sponsored by Hasset to commemorate his return and to appease his tenants. Will arrives and immediately recognizes Lewy among the "joyants." The shock of his arrest causes Lewy to counter with solemn warning for Cahill Fitzmaurice: "Tell Cahill I said, fot hurt was it to draw the blood of a little wether, in comparishum of an old friend's?—And see if Cahill will ask you what I mane, do" (*H*, 58). Not until this moment has either Lewy or his mother, old Vauria, who was on the deck of the hooker when Cahill knocked Aylmer overboard, thought of testifying against Cahill in a court of law. Will's act is to provoke such testimony in the final scene of the tale.

After the celebration ends and the peasants return to their mud cabins, Will goes to Kilavariga and Sandy proceeds to Bally-Aylmer: "Sandy had no wish to be overtaken by darkness on his way, in a country so haunted as his was with smugglers, peep-o'-day boys, fairies, ghosts, headless equipages, and revenue officers" (*H*, 61). He is not alarmed, however, when he is met by Will's father, Robert Aylmer.

The "ghost" survived the waters that night and has remained in exile fearing that Cahill has set the law upon him. He is now attempting reentry and Sandy is helping him. In this meeting Sandy informs his master that a friend is investigating the possibility of old Aylmer's safe return. When Sandy also tells Robert Aylmer that his son is becoming intimate with the daughter of his enemy, Aylmer swears to prevent the match and will use the law to achieve his end. Melodrama character-izes most of the concluding scenes.

The letter, intended to warn Will about Fitzmaurice, delivered coincidentally by its author to his son on the trail two nights before, and now returned once more to Will by Lewy during his arrest, is read the night of the celebrations by a curious young man. Signed simply by "an Ould follyer o the famalee," it warns Will to beware of Cahill Fitzmaurice and marriage to his daughter. Primed by the theme of the letter, Will is startled by the sudden appearance of a figure before him in his bedroom warning him to avoid Fitzmaurice and his daughter for the next two months, at which time he is to reappear.

The next morning Will attempts to jolt the truth from Cahill but fails to do so. Griffin describes the state of Will's mind: "The horror of his guardian's crime—the memory of all his kindness, pity for his pres-ent sufferings, and the natural instinct that prompted him to the course of justice, all contended for mastery within his soul, and made havoc of the region in their strife" (H, 74). Justice is being pursued on three sides now by Will, his father, and Lewy: Will's "evidence"—an anon-ymous letter and the report of an apparition—has turned his heart from one who has shown him charity; Lewy, a thief, has become some-thing far worse—an informer; Robert Aylmer seeks vengeance through the law as Cahill slowly and painfully confesses all to his daughter who in turn pledges undying devotion to God and to her father.

Griffin rushes to the final courtroom scene in which the chief witness for the prosecution of Cahill Fitzmaurice, in the case of the murder of Robert Aylmer, is the "deceased." Confronted by such histrionics, the lawyer for the crown throws his brief at the clerk after having accused a smiling judge of being "among the cabalists of Domdaniel" for his part in the outcome.

Melodrama presides in this early tale, but Griffin's use of dramatic structuring of scenes—the converging of Will's and his father's paths to the court, for example—his outlay of humor, and the vivid scenes of peasant realities make it effective entertainment. Griffin was appeal-ing to the rising middle class who were, in the main, his readers. He believed reform should start with them. Just as Will feels instinctively a need for justice or Kate cries out against a law that "persecutes after God has forgiven," Griffin preached for charity and an end to crippling pride.

He failed to create believable characters, however. Here is what happens to them: Will comes back to provincial Ireland and grows a little wiser in the knowledge of his people as he insists upon what has remained elusive for so long—justice; Kate loses her unpremeditated selfishness as she learns how much her God forgives, while Fitzmaurice and Aylmer, once fixed in the past with unrelieved consciences, are jarred back into the world of the present by two young people who want to shape a future for themselves with God and justice firmly in mind. All of this, however, remains quite superficial.

Will Aylmer, the central figure in the tale, merely reacts to what happens to him. He is part of a history of events. The only time the reader is given any knowledge of how his mind functions occurs during his initial meeting with Kate upon his return from Dublin. At first he is merely examining Kate's appearance and reacting to his naive preconceptions. In the remainder of the tale, however, he fails to live up to the potential that his closer observance of Kate displays. Further, he is never seen as a part of those qualities "of fire, of passion, of mirth, of thought, of feeling, or of fun" which he detects in Kate; instead, he is the recipient of her indignation when he denounces her father. Similarly, Kate does little to justify the intellectual strength she displays when first she notes the contradiction of studied carelessness in Will's appearance. Cahill remains hidden throughout the story: he was a smuggler and he is now a long-suffering recluse living with his only child.

Griffin's peasants are convincing in spite of their brief exposure. These are the people he knew best. His first "crathurs" no doubt pleased the young writer and he was soon to build on them: Sandy and Lewy become the brilliant characters Lowry Looby and Danny Mann of *The Collegians.* The middle men in "The Aylmers" are pale indeed: Hasset names a type and a place and Will apes unconvincingly the supposed manners and motives of a college student.

What Griffin does know intimately is the effect of the presence of British law in Ireland. He served as a court reporter in both England and Ireland and believed wholeheartedly in the reform that due process could achieve in his country. More familiar with the code that governed the Gaelic world, Griffin brings the two old Gaels together in a climax which points hopefully to a future time in Irish history

when justice and mercy will be realities in Irish courts of law. The
mentality of Robert Aylmer, who keeps himself in exile for ten years,
never once testing during the interval whether or not he could safely
return, matches that of his old partner in smuggling, who accepts the
appearance of his Gaelic community's rejection and never moves
beyond the first rebuff to reinstate himself. Such fatalistic behavior
seems characteristic of a people who have met injustice from the British government for centuries with either violence or passivity. When
the two meet in court it is a benevolent judge who perceives the humor
and tragedy in the case of Robert Aylmer, supposedly deceased, bringing the charge of murder against Cahill Fitzmaurice, and who is able
to restore some measure of reason to their distorted view of the world.
Undoubtedly, in all the trials Griffin witnessed as a court reporter, he
had met just such a model of British law in Ireland, a judge whose
compassion and understanding of the distinct character of the peasant
matched his own.

VI   "The Hand and Word": Summary and Analysis

In *Holland-tide,* six other stories follow "The Aylmers of Bally-Aylmer": "The Hand and Word," "The Brown Man," "Owney and
Owney-Na-Peak," "The Village Ruin," "The Rock of the Candle," and
"The Knight of the Sheep." Only one, "The Hand and Word," needs
commentary, since it presents Griffin as a developing novelist rather
than a folklorist. It is the tightly drawn, melodramatic love story of
Charles Moran and Ellen Sparling, who are driven apart by Ellen's
father, "a comfortable Palatine in the neighbourhood." They swear to
meet again in their niche atop the cliffs of Kilkee (now a resort town
in County Clare on the Atlantic coast). Pressed into service through the
influence of Mr. Sparling, Charles promises Ellen he will return in five
years' time. He gives his "hand and word" he will do so and takes her
hair ribbon to be used as a sign of his return.

Five years pass and Charles returns to his mother's inn where he
falls to playing cards with Yamon Macauntha, or Black Ned. Charles
cooly wins Yamon's money and proceeds that night to Ellen's home,
having sent the ribbon ahead by messenger to announce his arrival.
Yamon waits for him at the cliff's edge and hurls him to his death. At
the inquest Ellen notices that the button found in the corpse's hand
matches those of Yamon's coat, and when the murderer attempts
escape, he is forced to kill Ellen who relentlessly clutches at his throat.
In the chase that immediately follows, Yamon trips and topples head-

long over the cliff to his death. When some attention is given to the story's imagery, symbolism, peasants, themes, and unity, "The Hand and Word" becomes a fine example of Griffin's potential for prose.

Charles has never lived with the community and could not be expected to impress Ellen's socially aspiring parent. He perishes the night he returns from service after spending the evening gambling at his mother's inn, something she has acquired in five years through her industry. Thus, Griffin's moral involves the home life of each lover: in each case the parent, more concerned with his own material destiny, fails to provide the proper guidance for his child.

Charles and Ellen Sparling pledge their love at a cliff's edge. The cliff thus becomes a symbol of the basis upon which the lovers plan their uncertain future. Exile and return completed, Charles attempts to keep his word by meeting Ellen at the cliff site. Instead, he meets death at the hands of Yamon, who in turn goes to his death over the cliff.

The melodrama of such a structuring of events is partially concealed by the art of Griffin's description of a landscape which combines beauty and hazard for all who live there or are lured to the spot. Every detail needed to frame and to support the quick succession of events in the short story is carefully sketched in the opening pages so that the reader is able to follow the movements about to take place:

The most remarkable point of scenery about the place, and one with which we shall close our perhaps not unneedful sketch of the little district, is the Puffing-hole, a cavern near the base of the cliff . . . which vaults the enormous mass of crag to a considerable distance inland, where it has a narrow opening, appearing to the eyes of a stranger like a deep natural well. When the tremendous sea from abroad rolls into this cavern, the effect is precisely the same as if water were forced into an inverted funnel, its impetus of course increasing as it ascends through the narrow neck, until at length reaching the perpendicular opening of Puffing-hole, it jets frequently to an immense height into the air, and falls in rain on the mossy fields behind. (*H*, 125)

The peasant fishermen show the general level of Christian civilization and moral sensitivity in the community. Saving Charles's corpse "from the fishes" is the best they could do, all that the absence of law and order prompts them to do:

"We had been drawing the little canoe up hard by the cavern, seeing would we be the first to be in upon the seals when the hunt would begin, when I see a black thing lying on the shore among the sea-weed, about forty yards or upwards from the rock where I stood; and 'tisnt itself I see first, either, only two sea-gulls, and one of 'em perched upon it, while the other *kep* wheeling round above it, and screaming as nait'rel as a christen; and so I ran down to Phil, here, and says I: 'There's murder down upon the rocks, let us have it in from the fishes.' So we brought it ashore. 'Twas pale and stiff, but there was no great harm done to it, strange to say, in regard of the great rocks, and the place. We knew poor Moran's face, and we said nothing to one another, only wrapt the spritsail about it, and had it up here to Mr. Sparling's (being handier to us than his own mother's), where we told our story." (*H,* 146)

Immediately preceding the final tragic scene at the Sparling home where Charles's body has been brought by the fisherman and in which Ellen meets her death at the hands of Yamon, Griffin erringly provides a comic interlude. Terry Sparling, Ellen's brother, arrives at the home of the county coroner to summon him to the inquest:

When I say that an expression of involuntary satisfaction, which he in vain endeavoured to conceal, diffused itself over the tortuous countenance of the listener at this intelligence, it is necessary I should save his character by reminding the reader that he was a county coroner, and in addition to the four pounds which he was to receive for the inquest, there was the chance of an invitation to stay and dine with the Sparlings, people whose mode of living Mr. Morty had before now tried and approved.

"Come here, Terry, and take your morning," said he, filling a glass of ardent spirits, which the youth immediately disposed of with a speed that showed a sufficient familiarity with its use, although some affectation of mincing decency induced him to colour the delicious relish with a grimace and shrug of comical dislike, as he replaced the glass on the table. (*H,* 144)

Mr. Morty, the coroner, is a member of Ireland's rising, grasping middle class. His hypocrisy in acknowledging his call to duty is matched by that of the boy's feigned dislike of the liquor. Such compressed exposures of the middle class in this comic caesura are incisive enough to distract the reader's attention from the story's climax, thus rendering the final action—the death of both Charles's lover and his murderer—less effective a summation of the story's themes of vengeance, obedience, crime, and materialism.

The characters in this short tale are ensnared in melodramatic fits of dialogue, and moved along hurriedly to their tragic fates. However, in their brief exposure they seem sufficiently motivated and appear "real" in the sense that their lives are peculiar to the locale that Griffin describes so effectively. Taken together, "The Aylmers" and "The

Hand and Word" lend validity to the claim that Griffin's conversion from drama to prose was greatly facilitated by his efforts with shorter pieces. He neglects characterization in "The Hand and Word" in his outlay of landscape, action, dialogue, imagery, themes, symbols, morals, and humor. However, all the ingredients of this tale are so precisely balanced and thematically linked that Griffin had little space for melodrama as a vehicle for his preachment. "The Aylmers" attempts more and betrays more of this flaw.

The remaining five tales—"The Brown Man," "Owney and Owney-Na-Peak," "The Village Ruin," "The Knight of the Sheep," and "The Rock of the Candle"—are folktales, myths, and legends which Griffin offers as slight entertainments. However, with each one he never loses an opportunity to teach a moral.

For example, from his opening remarks in "The Brown Man" there is no mistaking the analogy between the Brown Man's devouring the flesh of his wife and England's tearing at the body of her sister isle. That the peasants of Ireland are the "salt" which preserves the teaching of the Catholic Church is apparent in "Owney and Owney-Na-Peak." With "The Village Ruin" Griffin shows the integrity of a myth and its relevance in his time: a leader must never relax in the performance of his duties. The last lesson taught by an embittered father to his sons—there shall be no legacy until death part us—in the folktale "The Knight of the Sheep" suggests Griffin's focus on the absolute aim of Christian education, the salvation of the soul. Finally, in the legend of "The Rock of the Candle," the theme of survival through thievery receives its earliest treatment in writing that was not so much the product of Griffin's creativity as it was of his remembering the many voices he heard when he visited and listened, before the small turf fires of Munstermen.[12]

The success of *Holland-tide* gave Griffin the incentive to continue in the genre, and, when *Tales of the Munster Festivals* appeared, he knew that the world's acceptance he so desperately had been seeking was close at hand.

CHAPTER 4

Tales of the Munster Festivals

I *The Theme of National Unity*

T HOMAS Flanagan states that Griffin's *Tales of the Munster Festivals* was one of the four books "which shaped, in important ways,
the nineteenth-century image of Ireland."[1] Griffin's main theme in the
Tales is national unity, certainly a theme of profound significance for
arbiters as well as readers on both sides of the Irish sea and one to
which he was to return in 1836 in *The Duke of Monmouth*. Feeling
deeply his country's problems in 1827, as he would in 1828 when he
wrote to Banim, "Give your leisure to England but reserve your health
and strength for your country and your friends,"[2] Griffin set to work
on his *Tales*. Within four months he wrote what would be a signifi-
cantly different book from the "sickly and sentimental garbage," as he
called it, which glutted the market. In the *Tales of the Munster Festivals* he called for moral discipline and national pride from his Irish
readers. From his foreign audience he desired that Ireland be known
for "the actual proportion" of her real life—her virtues as well as her
vices.

As he wrote his tales, Catholic emancipation was imminent. The
work of Grattan and O'Connell was spent on a people who had for
centuries been repelled by social injustice, economic suppression by a
"mother" country, oppression by absentee landlords, English persecution of a clergy who attempted to calm, educate, and aid the peasant
class, and the native pride and avarice of rising middle-class farmers
and merchants. Yet the kind of spirit which could bind the Irish anew
must transcend social, political, and economic ambitions as well as the
Irish tendency toward self-destruction. As social evaluator and moral-
izer, Griffin attempted to create a spirit of brotherhood, a theme
implicit in the dramatic structure of his tales and in the actions of his
characters.

Ireland's pride of families destroyed the possibility that a united social front would withstand coercion from without. Accepting home rule as a great part of Ireland's national destiny, Griffin concerned himself with the cure of those ills from within which enslaved and ravaged his people. He demonstrated through his art and instruction that those immoral and unlawful forces had their origin in pride and greed. Psychologically realistic character portrayals and thematic structuring of events pleaded for reform within his writing.

About the title, Daniel wrote: "The name was thought a good one, and had its origin in the design to include, in every tale, a description of some one of those festivals which are celebrated each by some traditional ceremony in the south of Ireland."[3] Griffin's purpose in such a "design" is one with the preacher's: the occasion to preach is the holy day; the method, equally appropriate, is to hold the glass up to life.

The thematic movements of characters in the three tales, "Card Drawing," "The Half Sir" and "Suil Dhuv," arise from descriptions of the social, religious, and economic aspects of their respective settings. "Card Drawing" begins on Candlemas Day as Duke Dorgan disembarks from a British naval vessel at Loop Head and sets out for his home. He bears with him Nelson's victory medal which sets the time of the tale close to the year 1805. Griffin takes the opportunity to describe the social structure of the inhabitants of southwest County Clare, those who lived immediately on the southern and easternmost shores of the Shannon. Of these he writes:

The coast is very thickly inhabited, and the people yet preserve in a great degree, the primitive and natural manners of their progenitors. They talk Irish—kill fish—go to sea in canoes—traffic in kind—eat potatoes and oaten bread—and exercise themselves in offices of kindness and hospitality towards strangers. This latter virtue has, however, in some parts of the region suffered injury from the efflux of bathers from the interior in the summer season, which taught them the use of convenience of ready money, in preference to their patriarchal modes of payment; and gave them, unfortunately, a more decided impression of its value than was consistent with the general character of Munster cottagers. The effect appears to have been similar to that which the liberality of English travellers has produced on the continent.[4]

Immediately to the west of the promontory and separated from it by a bay or large creek, is a community in remarkable contrast:

They are contradistinguished from Irish landholders in general by their apparent poverty and real wealth (many a tenant of clay walls being able

without much inconvenience to give a dowry of some hundreds to his daughter)—as well as by their want of curiosity in all speculative matters—and
their perfect unacquaintance with those popular themes of debate, which set
all the rest of the island by the ears. They till their gardens quietly, as their
fathers did before them—learn little and care for less—obey their priest in
all reasonable matters, and pay him like princes—go to market with their
oats and potatoes—eat—drink—dance—laugh—sleep and die. They have
no tyrants—no proctors—no middlemen—no demagogues—no meetings—
no politics. (*T*, 8)

Against the backdrop of these social and economic distinctions, Griffin
brings his hero Dorgan home seeking peace and happiness in his
homeland.

The locale for "The Half Sir" is Shanagolden on the southern shore
of the Shannon about twenty miles west of Limerick. It is the turn of
the century with the social order more commonly set between middleman in his castle and peasant in his mud hut. The central thematic
movement of Hamond is his return to Ireland to perform acts of charity among his people who are struck with disease and famine. Eugene
Hamond, the half-sir, constitutes a force for charity within a community which accepts his service and condemns his social status, that of
being a member of the newly rich. For "Suil Dhuv, the Coiner," Griffin selects the second decade of the eighteenth century to relate the
adventure of German emigrants from the Palatinate who have settled
in Munster. In this tale the principal movement concerns Issac Segur's
return from Germany, where he has been temporarily on business, to
Ireland in search of his daughter who has run off with the worthless
Dinny Macnamara. Griffin describes the Palatines: "Unmingled and
uninterested as the adventurers necessarily were with the politics and
the factious prejudices of the people, and having no internal or external
cause to divert them from the even course of steady and persevering
industry which their habits and inclination suggested to them as the
most likely to attain success, they were in every way prepared to take
advantage of the encouragements held out to them by the landed pro-
prietor" (*T*, 253). Thus, Griffin chooses communities polarized by their
hard lots to survive in periods of plague, lawlessness, political crises,
and insularity.

So much has to be remembered of the past and the present, Griffin
seems to say, to accomplish a national will to live with charity and good
will. Recognition of those foibles which can so readily create barriers
of hate and despair is the objective of every scene, every lesson of his

Munster tales. As highly dramatic as these scenes are, they not only entertain but also teach social unity to a country that had been ravaged by social disorder for over six hundred years. The misfits of all classes stand out as deterrents to national peace and harmony. Catholic emancipation, Griffin implies, begins with charity in the home.

Griffin begins the tales with a traveler-writer contemplating a visit to the Isle of Scattery from his position on the eastern shore of Poulnasherry Bay. Since he has to wait for a favorable tide, the traveler settles in the cottage of Patcy Magrath and is told the story of Duke Dorgan, whose widow has just left them free to talk. When Mrs. Magrath concludes, the traveler tells her that it would make an interesting tale. This comment draws a challenging reply from "a sour old man," who has all the while been poring over a tattered volume, that the traveler must know a great deal about telling the stories of the people of Ireland. The traveler claims he does and, wishing to analyze the antiquarian whose costume appears "to bear a close resemblance to some of the most antique of our national habiliments" (*T*, vii), he laments the fact that with so many writers employed in a commentary about the other parts of Ireland this part seems to have been left untouched. The old man is pleased that this is so in spite of the traveler's arguments that such publicity would serve to link Ireland with the rest of Europe, that one who tells their tales would be aiding the legislator and the judge who are so intimately connected with their lives. The old man refuses to have any of this: "You would, I suppose, have a typhus fever, or a scarcity of potatoes, remedied by a smart tale, while you would knock a general insurrection on the head, with a romance in three volumes!" (*T*, xi). Challenged by the traveler at this point to declare what he stands for, the antiquarian becomes Ireland of the past, present, and future:

"We are in no wise indebted to those writers, however brilliant their acquisition or endowments may be, who, professing to present faithful illustrations of the minds and hearts of our countrymen, greedily rake up the forgotten superstitions of our peasantry, and exhibit the result of their ungracious researches, the unhappy blemishes of our island, the weaknesses of our poor uninstructed peasantry, over which decency and good feelings would have thrown a veil, to the eyes of a world that, unfortunately, for us, is but too eager to seize every occasion for mockery and upbraiding against our forlorn and neglected country." (*T*, xi)

From such an assault upon his reason and feelings, the traveler resolves that his forthcoming volumes will speak to the antiquarian's point. He will bring "strong truth" and "instruction" to his tales. He will, as the old man exhorts him to, "deal fairly":

"Give our lights, if you will not overlook our shadows. . . . Have not our bogs and mountains their scenes of quiet contented virtue—of noble suffering—of generous forgiveness—of strong rude intellect and constant love, to match the "black attone" of turbulence—impatience—revenge—credulous folly, and licentious passion which you would attribute to them? Or if the idea of mirth and innocence, and milk and water be so closely associated in their eyes—let them turn to the Ireland that once *was*—and say, whether they cannot find there a theme worthy of the most splendid and varied capabilities." (*T*, xii)

Thus justification for the *Tales* becomes moral instruction, and the three novelettes which follow illustrate the truth of Gaelic Ireland.

II   *"Card Drawing": Summary and Analysis*

"Card Drawing" opens with Duke Dorgan's return from service in the British navy. He has served well, been provident, and now bears high prospects for a more successful attempt at winning the hand of Penelope McLoughlen from a father who has formerly denied an impoverished Dorgan. His arrival is watched by Pryce Kinchela, who at one time also desired to marry Pennie. The two greet each other as old friends and promise to meet again at the Bee-hive Inn. Dorgan sleeps that night in a hay-yard and upon waking the following morning hears a conversation between two women, a card-drawer or fortune-teller and Pennie McLoughlen, whose identity is disclosed neither to Dorgan nor to the reader at this time. The fortune-teller has just revealed to the maiden that her sweetheart is soon to return a rich man, and as the young girl disappears into the rushes to return home, Dorgan steps from concealment and is promptly persuaded to hear the news of his future. Although he professes nothing but scorn for what she unfolds, he is nonetheless somewhat disturbed by the dreadful fiction that he is to meet a violent end.

Duke proceeds to the Bee-hive Inn, meets Pryce, and while he drinks comments harshly upon Mr. McLoughlen's character only to be overheard and reprimanded by a clergyman. His sleep that night is turned fitful by the old fortune-teller's predictions of his "voylent" death. He awakes to apply a cold compress to his head by using an article of clothing. Unable to find any of his clothes in the dark, he once again returns to a restless sleep.

In the morning Duke sets out for Penelope's home, but as he approaches it, he notices a crowd of peasants milling about the entrance. The card-drawer suddenly appears at his side and tries to persuade him against entry. He nevertheless proceeds to the cottage and finds himself, in the midst of a coroner's inquest, identified as the murderer of his sweetheart's father.

The identity of the murderer is established by eyewitnesses: Pennie herself and McLoughlen's little niece (Mrs. Patcy Magrath who tells the story to the narrator) are compelled to recognize Dorgan's uniform and victory medal as the same items worn by the murderer. Actually, the night past, as Dorgan slept, Pryce borrowed uniform and medal for the murder and when he returned to his home after the murder, his mother immediately sensed a change in her only son while he himself was later subjected to a series of providential warnings that he must confess his guilt. After Dorgan's trial in Ennis, a town somewhat farther to the west, he is returned to Carrigaholt for hanging only to be saved by a last-minute confession from Kinchela.

Using the dramatic technique of setting upon the road together the returning hero and his bitter enemy, Griffin delineates the characters of both: the stark contrast between Dorgan and Kinchela, the former living a useful, patriotic, and profitable life in the service of his king, the latter, more in the service of his mother than anyone else, eking out a living from fishing and contraband activities. Dorgan returns to "forgive and forget" what has been done to him by a greedy, unsocial farmer. His service has made him whole. Pryce, on the other hand, appears "to be one of those beaten down characters, to whom degradation is so familiar, that they had rather lie tamely under the most contemptuous slights, than undergo the intolerable labour of supporting an independent and manly bearing" (*T*, 10). Griffin completes his contrast by the manner in which Dorgan withstands his trials and Kinchela crumbles under the onslaught of conscience.

The thematic rhythm which Griffin creates to launch and maintain his preachments is patterned in a dramatic, parallel structuring of scenes which finds Dorgan affected by the fraud of the card-drawer—and here Griffin builds on the psychological effects of long separation and of mounting fear to eclipse Dorgan's reason with superstition: Dorgan at the Bee-hive while he awaits Pryce's arrival, influenced by a scrapbook he peruses which contains a verse lamenting one who left

his native land "To soar at fame"; Dorgan with the help of Irish whiskey, loudly condemning Penelope's father within the hearing of a
priest who approaches to admonish him about the national propensity
among young men to darken character and to end their lives violently.
Finally, there is Dorgan's unrest after the whiskey and the outburst.

Kinchela's movements parallel those of Dorgan's. He meets twice
with Dorgan, the second time at the inn, where he takes full opportunity of the clergyman's presence to reopen the old wounds of his
intended victim and one-time rival. After the murder, there is Pryce's
fit of palpitations of the heart, the providential stone dropping from
the chimney narrowly missing crushing his skull, the confession he
makes in his fitful sleep, and the one he confides to Fed, a crony, about
the murder.

Especially effective is the scene in which Pryce has just made his
appearance at the home of the murdered farmer, when Pennie, in near
hysterics, falls at his feet, praising him for his power to forgive her
father. The clergyman, remembering Pryce's remonstrance to Dorgan,
adds to Pennie's praise. But Pryce is unable to handle this ironic turn.
He becomes agitated and pale, retreating hastily to the hills and to his
mother. What Pennie, the clergyman, and the entire community have
come to accept as truth is what most conveniently comes before their
eyes. No positive identification has been made of the murderer since
his face was blackened. Hence, a man slightly inebriated cries out
against a respected member of the community and his past becomes
his present; his doom seems inevitable to all who listened to him that
day at the inn.

If Pennie, the clergyman, and even his mother could never pene-
trate Kinchela's mask, his crony does. Fed says, "That I may be happy,
Kinchela . . . but you're just what I always took you for. You wor the
cruelest savage among us . . ." (T, 67), and it is not long before all come
to share Fed's knowledge.

As Kinchela dangles from the cliffs of Loop Head, filling his basket
with barnochs from the rocks, the rope crackles above his head signal-
ing disaster: "again all the horrors of the preceding night and morning
were renewed, and a stupifying terror seized upon his brain" (T, 74).
Fed manages to haul his companion up to the edge of the cliff whereupon Kinchela flees in the direction of his mother's house muttering
that God is impatient for his confession, that he must not be frightened
into confession this way lest there be no clemency from God. This has
been his third warning. Griffin tries to avoid the melodramatic in this
scene by making Pryce both the subject of it and an object within it as

he hangs from the cliff. He touches upon Kinchela's fear, and then by referring to some fishermen's unperceiving, "aboriginal" remarks to him as they pass below him in their canoes on their way home, Griffin succeeds in universalizing Kinchela's situation: as ignorant as the fishermen below Kinchela are concerning his danger so also are they, and all men, in complete ignorance of when their end may be met. In this last escape, Pryce understands the Almighty's mercy "which looked so lonely and beautiful amid the darkness and the multiplicity of his crimes" (*T*, 76).

In the scene following Kinchela's rescue Dorgan is being carted from his trial at Ennis back to his village of Carrigaholt for execution. As he is being taken away, the card-drawer tries to deliver a word to him but she is stopped: "'One word—O darlen sodger, don't kill me with the plundtherpush—Mr. Duke, keep up your sperrits—for there's one that'll—'" (*T*, 80). Whether she knows of Kinchela's impending confession or not, the reader never learns, but it is remarkable that Griffin credits peasant superstition to a point that even her return to the "faith" at story's end fails to diminish.

In the concluding scene of "Card Drawing," Griffin uses the same soldiers who first witness Duke's arrival at Loop Head to announce his arrival at the place of execution. The scene is also crowded with a cross section of the community: cottagers, fish-jolters, fishermen, members of the garrison, sheriff, magistrate, coroner, and priest, each to be remembered for his small part in the conviction of Duke Dorgan. The landlord, Mr. Madigan, is recalled by Dorgan when he first appeared at the Bee-hive: "This very landlord o' this publichouse I knew at school—a wild, scatterbrained young fellow . . . and to see him now enter the room, knocking the ashes off his pipe with the top of his little finger, hoping your honour is *convenient*, and talking of the duty on licenses and the distillery laws, as if he had never done anything since he was born but jug whiskey punch, and score double" (*T*, 34). At the trial, when he is called upon to verify Duke's presence at the inn the night of the murder, Mr. Madigan, in the affected phraseology of an emerging class, states that he is unable to do so. This Irish parvenu is matched in the narrator's commentary dealing with Pennie's father, farmer McLoughlen.

Mr. McLoughlen, who was about to bid on the property of an evicted farmer before he was murdered, offered Pryce a triple motive. McLoughlen's attitude had been changing about Dorgan, but his desire to expand his holdings at the expense of his neighbor never diminished. In this brief allusion to the violent work of the "Whiteboys," the marauding class of ruffians supposedly setting some things right in the war-torn land at the time, Griffin suggests, in parallel fashion, that the violence within individual hearts must be quelled together with the madness raging throughout an entire countryside. Griffin's example of how this peace is best achieved is in the person of Dorgan who has learned to correct his own errant ways in disciplined service. Not much more of the class is considered in this tale, apart from mention that another farmer is too busy to watch the hanging.

The coroner, an official of the court, has been crisp and effective in his handling of Dorgan. He admonishes the accused often enough and always with the air of greatest certainty about his guilt. It is the priest who acts so decisively in the melodramatic hanging scene. His power and influence halt the hanging at the last possible moment when he insists that the executioner perform his duty and not leave it to his assistant, a boy. In this instance of slight moral direction, Pryce comes forth, shouting to be heard. Overruling the objection of the sheriff, the priest summons Pryce to him with the same air of authority with which he reproved Duke earlier at the inn and later testified against him at the murder scene: he directs "justice" with the aplomb of a card-drawer as Dorgan awaits God's will with strength and control.

The moral force of the *Tales* rests basically on the high value Griffin places in the relation of parent to child. Such endorsement of the parent-child relationship is demonstrated in the awry relationship Pryce shares with his aged mother who believes that her son is both pious and honest, and who never suspects that his smuggling is supplying her with Christmas and Easter dues and the usual present of candles for the altar. She is oblivious to the economics involved in her worship and so given over to her religion that she has failed to understand her son. Provoked by the murder of old McLoughlen, she reacts: "Woe and sorrow! . . . when will they be weary of drawing the blood of the gray-headed? Your own father, Pryce, died by the cold steel. It is true for the priest what he said from the altar last Sunday, that Ireland was more cursed by the passions of her own children than ever she was by Dane or Sassenagh" (*T*, 62). But it is clear to the reader that telling Mrs. Kinchela the truth about "passions" has given her little knowledge of how to detect them in her son. And there is Penelope and her father, who so brutally refuses the marriage proposals of both Duke and Pryce. McLoughlen, in his zeal for getting on, has dismissed Dorgan instead of offering him an opportunity to better himself.

The "heroic generosity" of Dorgan in forgiving his lover for her lack of faith in him is a plea for national unity, poignant in the context of

Catholic emanicipation. The narrator comments: "If the frame-work of human character were not composed of the same materials through all classes, what hope could we have that the rich, the elegant, and the highborn, would honour with their sympathy the pictures of humble sorrow and affection, which these Tales are intended to present?" (*T*, 60). Thus, justification for the *Tales* becomes moral instruction.

The melodrama of "Card Drawing" is made more palatable by recurring motifs from *Holland-tide* (for instance, Griffin's continued use of the cliff) which tend to expand Griffin's art and didacticism through more effective characterizations. Dorgan and Kinchela, though stock contrasts, are delivered with more force and effect in the multiple viewing which Griffin brings to the story. They view a community; a community views them. They reveal their inner thoughts during moments of extreme physical and mental stress and the reader receives, in total effect, a comprehensive view of a society of peasants, priests, and middlemen, highly believable in their moral and immoral behavior. They are, however, just one of many communities and typify the paradox and tragedy of Ireland: in a country attempting to establish a national identity, they tear themselves to pieces from within through crimes ranging from petty jealousies to murder on the grand scale, the "Whiteboys'" scale.

Dorgan's return is reminiscent of Will Aylmer's from *Holland-tide*. The structure of scenes set in motion by the return of central figures in Griffin's tales begins to signal the emergence of realistic characters. Will Aylmer returns to find justice for his father in the chaos of his Kerry neighborhood; Dorgan learns the value of his self-discipline when unjustly accused of murder by his former neighbors; Eugene Hamond of "The Half Sir," a self-exile now returned, faces the scorn of those he aids. In these confrontations of his main characters Griffin hopes to create events which will help uncover both their own weaknesses and strengths and those of their neighborhood.

III *"The Half Sir": Summary and Analysis*

"The Half Sir" deals more with the "Rich, the elegant, and the high-born," and, more precisely, with the individual who comes to his wealth suddenly, without the history and the pride of family that a populace can revere. The cycle of life implicit in the themes of ambition, pride, exile, and regeneration constitutes the moral structure of Griffin's scenes, causing the separation and eventually effecting the rec-

onciliation of his protagonists Emily Bury and Eugene Hamond. After
setting the stage for the moment of their reunion with a highly effective dramatic opening in chapter 1, Griffin devotes the remaining eight
chapters to establishing the sequence of events that led to and followed
the breakup of the lovers.

As in so many of Griffin's tales, the exile-return theme plays an integral part in the dramatic, moral structure of "The Half Sir." The plot
summary which follows attempts to show how Griffin, at age twenty-
three, has enlarged his perspective of fiction to include greater treatment of the near contemporary social scene. Hamond's return to an
impoverished and famine-stricken Munster and his example of charity
is, so far, Griffin's finest example of the alliance of art and morality.

"The Half Sir" begins with the Wren-boys of Shanagolden, a small
village in County Limerick, forming their "little rustic procession" to
serenade the "fair ladies," Misses Falahee and Bury, at the home of
Mr. Falahee. Emily Bury is about to present herself to Hamond as Miss
O'Brien, a friend of his lost lover. This subterfuge for the purpose of
reconciling the lovers is all rather good-naturedly arranged by Emily's
dear friend, Martha O'Brien, who is happily married to Mr. Hunter,
the local magistrate.

After the Wren-boys conclude their serenade, Mr. Falahee asks if
they have been to Castle Hamond. In the discussion which follows, the
reader learns that a distinction has to be made between a true gentleman, like Mr. Falahee, and a half-sir, such as Eugene Hamond who
possesses neither the generosity of a true gentleman nor the family
background of one, that being well established in the time-honored
preoccupation with hunting, gaming, and drinking. The impact of this
discussion is felt keenly by Emily, who loses no time in reminding all
that Mr. Hamond, a somewhat eccentric recluse, is, nevertheless, one
of the most zealously charitable members of the community, working
tirelessly for sick and poor. The following scene is set at Castle
Hamond, and a dialogue between Hamond and his man Remmy
O'Lone prepares the reader for the reception the Wren-boys are to
receive on this St. Stephen's Day from Hamond who is not only a Protestant half-sir but a descendant of Cromwell as well. Following the
Wren-boys is Mr. Hunter who will present Emily incognito to her former lover. And here, Griffin begins his flashback.

As a child Eugene is left in the care of his deceased father's second
cousin, an old man just returned from America with a fortune. The
sensitive child's education under the direction of this old man precludes any chance for normal development, and, with his religious and

social background, young Hamond finds himself ill at ease in the company of the formidable "true" gentry. His lessons in class consciousness are painful to such a point that when he finds himself engaged to the beautiful, coquettish Emily Bury, he thinks it nothing less than miraculous. However, the engagement is broken when Emily abuses the service of Remmy, Hamond's man.

Emily marries politically aspiring Lord E———, who falters in his climb to power and subsequently dies. Meanwhile, Hamond has set off on an extended world tour with Remmy. Chastened by the years of travel and exile, he returns to his neighborhood to take up the work of charity: famine is prevalent, the Wexford Rebellion has begun, and service to the people becomes his only concern.

Hamond works among the diseased and poor until he falls ill and is nursed back to health by Emily whose identity remains unknown to him through his delirium. Emily also has been aiding the sick. Changed considerably from the coquette of Dublin society she once was, she now wishes to meet Hamond, and so her friend Martha O'Brien Hunter arranges the rendezvous and reconciliation by having her husband call at Hamond Castle on St. Stephen's Day.

Griffin's story of Christian charity receives its initial impetus in the opening scene. He focuses immediately upon the classes—the Catholic gentry, Mr. Falahee; the Protestant half-sir, Eugene Hamond; the aspiring middleman, Mr. Charles Lane, who ludicrously affects English speech and manners; Terry Lenigan, leader of the Wren-boys; and Emily Bury, who embodies the spirit of Ireland emancipated from destructive pride.

The dialogue between Falahee and Lenigan defines the class of half-sir. Falahee has just been told that a half sir "has got no blood in him." Terry continues: "No an; any more than meself. A sort of a small gentleman, that way: the singlings of a gentleman, as it were. A made man—not a born gentleman. Not great, all out, nor poor, that way intirely. Betuxt and betune, as you may say. Neither good pot-ale, nor yet strong whiskey. Neither beef nor vale. Castle Hamond! What's Castle Hamond to me as long as the master wouldn't conduct himself proper!" (*T*, 101–2). Emily questions Lenigan and wrings from him the admission that Mr. Hamond had "religion" and charity, but no "heart," that is to say, Hamond does not drink, hunt, or gamble. Emily has made her point but to no apparent effect upon Lenigan. Turning from the window at which she has been addressing him in the street below, she is met once more by Mr. Lane, who is trying desperately to impress her with his newly acquired English manners.

Mr. Lane, unaware that his pretentious ways are the cause of his trouble with Emily, struggles "to shake off the secret yoke which the good lady had, quite unconsciously, cast upon him; his struggles served only to make him feel the weight of his fetters more severely" (*T*, 106). Griffin's point is this: an individual's pride must be directed to serve humanity before he and his country can be made whole. Lenigan and the boys want liquor and songs; Lane wants to be accepted as an "equal" by a person who shows him no respect but to whom he is nevertheless mysteriously attracted. Emily's attraction is a spirit within her, one for all of Ireland, which is synonymous with service to God and to humanity.

The Wren-boys' procession next moves to Castle Hamond. Their singing cues Remmy's appearance: "It was a hatchet-face, with a pair of peeping pig's eyes set close (like a fish's) on either side—the mouth half open, an expression of mingled wonder and curiosity depicted on the features—and a brown strait-haired wig, which time had reduced to a baldness almost as great as that of the head which it covered, shooting down on each side, like a bunch of rushes, toward the shoulders" (*T*, 109). Singularly impressive in the peasant grotesque is his spirit of service and loyalty to the Protestant half-sir which is felt in the dialogue immediately following Remmy's comic interlude with the Wren-boys, who fail to secure a drop of cheer for all their efforts. Hamond asks what he, a Protestant, has to do with St. Stephen's Day. Remmy's reply carries an analogy for Ireland's fate under British rule: the wren is king of the birds because he has stolen under the wing of the eagle who soared high for the crown and lost when, after flying as high as he could, the little wren flew higher. The significance of the bird explained, Hamond reaffirms his alienation from such superstition and ritual, and Remmy remains secure in his own position of wren.

Griffin, through a series of opening scenes and dialogues, places his hero in the perspective of an "alien" working charitably within a community which accepts his charity but fails to comprehend the man. Through flashbacks, the reader comes to learn about this benevolent "alien" whose "history of feelings" begins when he first enters his foster parent's home. The ambition, vanity, and selfishness of Hamond's foster parent prey upon the sensibilities of the child who becomes confused and morbid because the old man's fits of generosity and abuse follow so closely, one upon the other. As he grows older his shyness deepens since communication with the old man is now nearly impossible. Quite unexpectedly one day, the boy is told to forget his peasant companion Remmy O'Lone and to go to Dublin to complete an education, "slick-right-away."

The old man's detestation of the law, a trait which Griffin marks as "almost national in certain parts of Ireland," has also been a debilitating influence for Eugene. So great is the old man's fear of having anything to do with the law that he signs his entire estate over to Eugene before he dies, making the transaction as simple as possible, for himself. One final request is made of Eugene by the old man who lies dying: Eugene must go out into the world and practice charity, something his guardian has been unable to do. The old man acquired wealth in America under brutally competitive circumstances. The experience broke his charity with the world, but he is able to make this tremor of conscience the most important part of Eugene's legacy.

When Eugene first meets Emily Bury, some time after he has completed his studies in Dublin, his uncle's injunction produces significant results. Eugene's rigid sense of justice causes him to put aside his desire for Emily when she cruelly assaults the dignity of his friend and servant Remmy O'Lone. At this point Griffin comments upon a national distinction drawn between the Irish and the English: wealth in England, says Griffin, facilitates passage from one class to another whereas in Irish circles of fashion no such guarantee or facility exists: "Pride—mere family pride, is one of the grand national foibles which yet remain unbroken by the inroads of modern intelligence; and no internal or external wealth with which a man may be gifted in his own person, will compensate for the mental or corporeal poverty of his ancestors" (*T*, 133). In Ireland, the quality of a man's ancestors determines his position in society for life regardless of his efforts to change it.

With a large measure of ancestral poverty, Eugene finds himself in the company of Emily Bury and her friends. Pairs of opposites are presented by the narrator: Martha O'Brien, blonde and sedate; Emily Bury, dark, restless. Dialogue soon discloses Emily's intolerable pride as she passes upon Mr. O'Neil, a "true Irishman": "There never was a man who lived so entirely upon the possession of his friends as Mr. O'Neil. He is a poor man himself, he admits, but then he is the poorest of his own family—he is an uninformed blockhead, he will allow you, but then he has such 'bright' people, relatives of his—he does not deny that he is a worthless, dissipated wretch—but all the rest of his family are so respectable and so high-minded—In fact, you would think, to hear him speak, that he was proud of being the scape-grace of his own house—the only black sheep in the fair flock of the white-fleeced O'Neils" (*T*, 136). This "black sheep" and Emily together humiliate Hamond to the point that he confesses "that for the interests of society in general, and for those of morality and of religion itself, it would be much better that all men should remain in that rank in which they were born or at least that nothing less than a development of capabilities, absolutely wonderful, should entitle them to seek a place above their fathers" (*T*, 143). This thought from the graceful, intelligent, handsome young half-sir juxtaposed with the pride of O'Neil, who counts it a good day when a relative snubs him at the Castle, prepares the way for Hamond's withdrawal. His loss of Emily and his subsequent world travels signal the beginning of the development of his wonderful "capabilities," while Emily's pride soon leads her into an unfortunate marriage to Lord E——, who, before his untimely death, abandons his bride to sit in the British Parliament where "he did not scruple putting his honour 'to nurse' in the lap of the reigning minister" (*T*, 177).

During this interval of Emily's suffering and loss, Hamond and Remmy have been abroad and now are dramatically reintroduced as two travelers returning to their native soil. Their haggard expressions and shabby dress denote long, hard travel, but the somber theme of exile and return receives a comic rise before it settles on the home scene of famine, plague, and rebellion.

As Hamond lies below the deck of the hooker, Remmy speaks with the forecastle man:

> "It's wet you are, I'm in dread," said the forecastle man, with an air of mock concern.
>
> "A trifle that way," replied the other, with a tone of seeming indifference—and adding, as he composedly applied his handkerchief to the dropping breast of his coat—"Only av all the Munster boys wor nuvur to be *drier* than what meself is now, twould be a bad story for the publicans."
>
> "Why thin, I see now," said the boatman, assuming at once a manner of greater frankness and good-will, "that you *are* a raal Irishman after all, be your taken a joke in good parts."
>
> "In good parts!—In all parts, I'm of opinion," replied the passenger merrily, extending his arms to afford a full view of his drenched figure. (*T*, 181)

Moments later the hooker's captain and Remmy speak on the subject of English aid to Ireland. The captain uses an old fable to make a point: England is likened to "Congcullion" who is sent for by the king of Ulster to deliver him and his men from the peril of an old hag who sits atop a tower showering arrows upon them. "Congcullion" shoots her down but in her fall she strikes and kills one of the king's best men. The king is displeased to the point of wishing that "Congcullion" never answered the call. "It's the same way with the English when they try to do good for uz here in Ireland," says the captain. Remmy is more positive in his thinking: "but still in all it's a great thing for 'em to mane well any way, bekays be that mains there's hopes they'll be set right one time or another, you see" (*T*, 187). Setting things right is Hamond's mission: Remmy and he were recently in London where Hamond had been appointed by the government to distribute money to the poor, "by raison of the great rain that was last year, that pysin'd all the skillaans in the airth, which the English (an sure it's a new story with 'em) subscribed for 'em—an sure 'twas good of 'em for all," says Remmy (*T*, 184).

Griffin's treatment of national character and history expands rapidly from this point forward as themes of famine, plague, poverty, and law-lessness are loosed dramatically upon the two travelers who begin the last phase of their journey home. From a hill overlooking the road upon which Hamond and Remmy are traveling, a shot, delivered apparently by a member of the "Whiteboys," narrowly misses Remmy and the occupants of a coach who have come abreast of the exiles. Remmy immediately goes to the assistance of the gentleman and his lady, fawning over them much of the time and to the great displeasure of Hamond: "It is thus that the services of the poor are always valued. No matter what the sacrifice may be—of personal safety—of toil—of health—of heart's ease and all self-interest, the high-born ingrate thinks he is more than quit of all obligation, by flinging it too, as that man did, at his feet—not to be taken from the earth without defiling his fingers" (*T*, 193). The gentleman happens to be Magistrate Hunter with his wife, Martha, who, according to Remmy's account, shows the greater calm through the whole incident. The attempted assassination moves Hamond to resolve to fulfill as much of his neglected duty as time will allow, for, he says, "happiness is a gift which a man may want himself and yet bestow" (*T*, 195). The attempt on the magistrate's life is Griffin's single note of the presence of the "Whiteboys." Their violence is to be viewed more closely in "Suil Dhuv," the concluding tale.

As Hamond makes his pledge to dedicate himself to the poor, a beggar approaches asking for tobacco. His ravaged appearance so appalls Hamond that he questions the fellow about additional needs he may have, whereupon the half-sir learns of the charitable works of a Miss

O'Brien (actually Emily Bury working her charity under an assumed name) and of the intolerable conditions under which the diseased peasants are left to die in the fields by their unafflicted neighbors. The beggar's family manages to survive in its present state because of the English, who according to the wretch, send "potaties, an male moreover."

As he continues on his journey, Hamond views scenes of suffering and deprivation which he has never encountered in the novels of his day on Irish suffering:

Numbers of poor wretches, who seemed to have been worn down by the endurance of disease and famine to the very skeleton, were dispersed through the fields, some of them occupied in gathering nettles, the common food of the people for a long period, and *prishoc* weed from the hedges, for the purpose of boiling, in lieu of a more nutritious vegetable. The usual entreaties, and their accompanying benediction that "the Lord might save him from the sickness o' the year," were multiplied upon his path as he proceeded. The red crosses which were daubed on almost every cabin door as he passed, and the sounds of pain and sorrow which came on his hearing from the interior, afforded him a fearful evidence of the extent to which the ravages of the disease had been carried—a disease attended by a peculiar malignity in its application to Ireland; for it was seldom fatal in itself, but merely disabled the unhappy countryman (whose sole hope of existence depended on his being left the use of his arms) for a few weeks, until the season for exertion had gone by, and then left him to gasp away his life in the pangs of the famine which was consequent on his involuntary remissness. The tillage, except where the indications of unusual wealth and comfort shewed that it was the property of a considerable holder, bore marks of haste and negligence, and altogether the general appearance of the country was affected in no light degree by the misery of its inhabitants. (*T*, 203–4)

Griffin closes the gap between Hamond and Emily when the half-sir becomes a victim of the disease he is fighting. In his delirium Emily's real presence is blurred by the sick man's hallucinations, and the whole scene suggests the predicament of Irish suffering. How difficult it is, Griffin seems to say, for an ailing person or nation to distinguish reality from appearance. Reigning melancholy, disease, poverty, lawlessness, and ignorance seem invincible foes to life-giving charity.

Education and moral instruction are integral in any attempt at establishing charity in the mind of a peasant or a gentleman, and instruction is what Hamond receives when his fever passes. Minny O'Lone, Remmy's aged mother, advises Hamond to go to church and to make amends for his past ways. The severity of her direction is followed by a humorous tale of penance and reform, the moral of which reminds Hamond of his early dedication to charity. The physical strength that now returns to his body is accompanied by a more profound awareness that he is alive to do God's will.

Eugene Hamond's final instruction comes from Emily in their meeting at Hunter's home. Posing as Mrs. O'Brien, a friend of Hamond's former lover, Emily proceeds to speak about the subject of retreat from the world of action. Hamond is startled by the subject's application to himself, and, when Emily finishes telling the story of her own wasted life, she is overcome by her own feelings of guilt which have surfaced once more. The entire confession on the nature of coquetry causes Hamond to recoil in recognition of his lost lover and the melodramatic scene closes upon Emily's words: "And advise our neighbours to take warning by our tale," said Emily, "and to be convinced that they can be all that true Irish men and women ought to be; that they may retain Irish spirit—Irish worth—and Irish honour, in all their force, without suffering their hearts to be warped and tainted by the vapours of IRISH PRIDE" (*T*, 244). Not long after the reunion their marriage is celebrated, and Castle Hamond becomes a center of happiness and charity for family and neighborhood.

From the sheep-stealers of the Kerry hills in "The Aylmers" of *Holland-tide* to the "tolerable faithful picture of a Munster cottage life" in the *Tales*, Griffin expands his presentation of the social turmoil he knew through personal observation. Characters now seem to be more believable. Will Aylmer, an orphan at the time he is sent to Dublin for an education, is pale in comparison to Hamond, also an orphan, whose character is more fully delineated in terms of his childhood experience with a neurotic guardian. Hamond's diffidence and pride, for example, before Emily's Dublin coterie is understandable because of his old uncle's warped view of reality. In "Suil Dhuv," Issac Segur's return to his adopted homeland and his search for his daughter are a continuation of Griffin's development of the exile-return theme in which dramatic, moral structuring of scenes leads to more psychologically penetrating characterizations and a heightening of moral force.

IV *"Suil Dhuv": Summary and Analysis*

Social verisimilitude abounds in this concluding tale of a daughter's disobedience to her parent. Sally Segur has defied her father in her elopement with Dinny Macnamara, whom old Issac has come to condemn for his errant ways. While old Segur was in Germany on business, Sally joined Dinny who had by then become "Suil Dhuv" ("Black Eye"), the forger and the leader of a lawless band who made crime a way of life in these Penal times.

The story begins with the return of Segur to his adopted home in search of his daughter. When he stops for a night's lodging, it is Sally who greets him. She and Dinny have assumed the name of Spellacy and are operating the inn as a screen behind which the criminal activities of Suil Dhuv are in full operation. Upon recognition of his daughter, the old man demands to know the whereabouts of Dinny, who has planned for an evening's work the looting of a church and the abduction of Lilly Byrne, a local beauty.

Dinny and Segur meet, finally, as the penitential fires of the faithful peasants burn in the hills on this St. John's Eve. Here, Segur, acting as judge and executioner, slays Dinny.

When Segur is joined shortly by Shine, a minister of the Church of Ireland, and Abie Switzer, a peasant, the reader receives his first flashback as the old man divulges the purpose of his travel to his companions. He begins his story with the arrival of Dinny Macnamara at the Segur farm and his subsequent love affair with Sally, old Segur's daughter. The narrator carries the story to the point of Sally's disappearance while Segur is in Germany on business. Mr. Shine has remained curious and attentive; however, the prospects of refreshment at some nearby inn are growing increasingly inviting for the divine, so much so that when they are suddenly met by Awney Farrel, the hedge scholar, who suggests that the party stop at Spellacy's inn close at hand, Mr. Shine is first to put spurs to his horse.

From the point of Segur's arrival at the inn to the tale's conclusion on the hillsides of Drumscanlon at the moment of the lighting of the fires on St. John's Eve, the drama intensifies in the scenes at the inn's forge and once again upon the road. At the inn all the main characters meet. As the old man sleeps, Mrs. Spellacy (Sally) attends him until her cry of recognition startles the company and betrays her identity to her father who refuses to acknowledge her under the circumstances of their present meeting. Nevertheless, Sally is not to be put off. She poses as a friend of Sally before the company and tells the story of pride which has brought ruin to the Palatine's daughter. In spite of the obvious remorse Sally's review of her past sins displays, Segur continues his refusal to recognize his daughter until the final scene in which he kills Dinny.

Before the action leaves the inn, the following scene takes place between Awney Farrel and Mr. Shine. In it Griffin makes his point about the Church of Ireland and the poor of Ireland. The minister has been stuffing himself with food and informing both Awney and Dinny's child about the affairs of one Jonathan Swift, "Who hath employed a portion of time which he might have turned to far better uses, in composing certain ridiculous verses for the service of the nursery—replete with nothing salutary or instructive—" (*T*, 316). Ironically, Shine's instruction is about to begin in the matter of dealing with buried "treasure." Before this occurs, however, Awney's aside to the child proves apt mimicry:

"Look at de gentlemen—now—do—who is dat? who is dat here? What's dat? What do you say? O you tief! He's aten all de beef and de mutton intirely, is he? O, have manners, master! O fie, Sir! Av he ates de mutton, he has de money to pay for it, and dat's what he got be his learnen—be his minden his A, b, ab, an his e, b, eb—an his b, a, baa, and his b, e, bay—and every whole tote dat way. And do you mind 'em, Sir, and you'll be like him, haven money to spend for what you like best, and enoof o' dat to lave for de smart boy dat would be showen you over de wild mountain in an evenen, and would be hungry for his dinner may be, and not haven de price of it in his pocket—so he wouldn't—" (*T*, 319)

Sally's cry of recognition of her father is enough to turn the minister from his plate. Then:

The preacher turned round, while his eyes were still directed in amazement toward the parlour, to the thin-faced lad. He found the latter, however, had been much more profitably occupied than in attending to the preceding scene. He had slipped quietly into the preacher's chair, and busied himself with the utmost eagerness in completing the task which the other had left unfinished.
"Eat, friend," said the preacher, after pausing and staring on the lad for a few moments. "Eat, and be filled. Let no respect of persons abash or trouble you in the performance of a needful duty." (*T*, 323)

As Awney tends to his "needful duty," Dinny leads Robert Kumba to the forge and, once inside, leaves him in a position to observe all as he addresses his men. Kumba has been one of Dinny's sources of income ever since the wily peasant has convinced the middleman that he can restore to him his lover, Lilly Byrne. Lilly's father has renounced Kumba for his past dissipation with Macnamara. When Dinny reveals the fact that the gang intends to raid Lilly's home in

Drumscanlon, Kumba falls from the loft, is captured, and then left
guarded by Red Rody, one of Dinny's men. In Kumba's escape Rody
is killed, and the old murderer's dying words serve to evoke images of
how his breed operates outside the law. Griffin provides his own commentary on the nature of Irish crime:

> There is a proverb current among the Irish peasantry, which, as we have
> not been in the habit of obtruding these aphorisms of vulgar wisdom upon
> him hitherto, the reader will excuse our transcribing. It runs, in English,
> something in this way—"Carry a goat to the chapel, and he never will stop
> until he mounts the altar." The truth of the axiom is more frequently exem-
> plified in the annals of Irish crime, than, perhaps, in those of most other
> nations. The reason of this may be found in the simple fact, that Irish crime,
> like Irish virtue, is not the creature of the mind but of the heart. They are a
> people more frequently betrayed into guilt by the impulses of strong feeling,
> than the cold suggestions of convenience, and in proportion to the violence
> of the stimulus applied, will be found the depth and atrocity of the outrage
> that is committed. (*T*, 385–86)

What propels Dinny to the chapel and its desecration in one of the
final scenes of "Suil Dhuv" is the cumulative effect of his strong hatred
for a society which betrayed him at birth by its very chaotic nature.
His violence and rage are set in motion by the blow he receives as he
is driven from its limits. Griffin speaks of crime in terms of a goat in
a chapel and then leaves his reader with the chapel scene for final,
private musing.

Segur's premediatated crime is about to take place and Sally knows
it. She also knows her husband will never accept surrender and so,
before Segur leaves the inn for the forge, he receives an ambivalent
plea from his daughter. Tortured by the thought that any harm might
come to her father or her husband, she cries: "All I entreat is that you
will not fire—oh—do not! until you are compelled" (*T*, 362). When
Segur arrives at the forge with Shine and Abie in pursuit of Dinny,
they are met by Cuthbert Byrne, one of a class of rising middlemen
the author spends considerable space in exposing to his readers. Byrne
is a grazier:

> . . . an elderly-looking, *dressy* sort of man, equipped at all points, to *an agony*
> of elegance, and standing (a coarse, ill-fashioned block of clumsy vulgarity)
> in the midst of a blaze of finery, looking like a black ragged cloud in a sunny
> sky—or a draught of muddy inn-keeper's wine, in a gold tankard (traveller's
> fare) presenting, as he crept out of the midst of a cloud of black smoke, which

issued with him through the low battered door of the forge, the most apt illustration that could be desired of the hedge school doggerel—

> "A man without learning, and wearing fine clothes,
> Is like a pig with a gold ring in his nose." (*T*, 364)

This ludicrous figure is responsible for a great deal of the suffering among the dispossessed farmers of Munster, and although Griffin makes no direct allusion to the fact that graziers become rich at the expense of thousands of homeless peasant farmers, the implication seems apparent in the grotesque image he projects of the plunderer.

Byrne happens to be Lilly's uncle, and when he learns from Segur what "Suil Dhuv" intends to do at Drumscanlon, the party sets off, and Griffin draws his characters closer in two contrasting movements. As an approaching storm closes in on Cuthbert's party, the "buck" from Cork offers his "loody" to Sally who has just joined them with Robert Kumba. They hurry on and it soon becomes obvious to Kumba that Cuthbert's "blather" is about his own Lilly Byrne.

The weather which marks Dinny's progress is quite fair, and the countryside he surveys reminds him of the past and of some of the good things that happened to him as a child. The familiar country scene and the past kindnesses of Segur and Sally begin to work upon Dinny's conscience as he and Mun Maher leave the band temporarily to plunder a nearby church. Dinny posts Maher as lookout. Approaching the church he meets an old woman who blesses him for helping her over a stile.

Robbery and sacrilege are now so formidable that Dinny is barely able to function. Griffin dwells on the physical and psychological aspects of Dinny's crime by instructing his readers in all that is happening to Macnamara:

... long habit of self-willed contempt for, and obstinate resistance to the truth of religion is often apt to substitute a mechanical superstition in its place; so it might now be observed of the stained and hardened soul that stood, with the purpose of the last of human offences—black, daring, deadly sacrilege— before the door of the temple, that the fouler and fiercer his resolution became, the more weak and nervous was his frame, and the more fearfully active his memory and his imagination. The short, quick breathings of the wind through the dry thatch made him start and tremble, while sudden forms, of he knew not what or whom, seemed to flit before and about him, through the evening gloom. . . . He trembled violently, flung himself unconsciously on his knees—struck his breast rapidly and violently with his

clenched fist—muttered a hurried snatch of the half-forgotten rosary—and
yet, by some strange influence, amid all this agitation and remorse, the
thought of desisting from the crime, which he meditated at that very
moment, scarcely once occurred to him. . . .

The sudden dash of the waters behind him began to boom upon his hearing, like the sound of distant thunder.—He struck fiercely at the lock of the
door, then started and trembled as the many echoes of the blow came back
upon him from the rents and hollows of the cliff and glynn—and again
repeated the strokes with double vehemence. At length, flinging the hammer
away, he stept a few paces back—then dashing himself furiously against it,
he sent it crashing round upon its hinges. . . . The whole proceeding, from
this moment, was one of such absolute delirium, that he could hardly be said
to have acted it with consciousness. He rushed to the recess in which the
object of his search—the silver chalice or ciboreum,—was kept, forced it
open, flung himself on his knees once more, clasped his hands, prostrated
himself on the earth, started to his feet, snatched the sacred vessel, dashed
the contents, the sight of which almost maddened him, upon the altar—and
fled in an abandonment of utter fear along the aisle, panting heavily, crossing
himself, and striking his breast, and muttering prayers and curses blended—
while his sight swam and wandered wildly over the place, his ears seemed to
ring with the din of mingled thunders, hymns and laughter; flakes of whitish
light darted with throbs of anguish from his eyeballs; the air about him grew
hot and suffocating; the darkening vault of the night seemed to press with a
horrid weight upon his brain; and his conscience, rising like a buried giant,
from beneath the mountains of crime, he had cast upon it, revealed, and
almost realized the Pandemonium which his slighted, though unforgotten
faith had pointed out to him, with a warning finger in his days of early innocence. (*T*, 400–02)

Such didacticism needs relief and Griffin provides it in the person of
the old woman Dinny helped over the stile. She now approaches Mun
Maher, her son, who awaits Dinny's return, and the clout she delivers
to him in no way suggests the debility which prompted Dinny's charity: "You contrairy boy! have I found you at last? Get up with you, and
coom along him wit me this minnit, I tell you agin!" (*T*, 407). But Mun
can do no such thing. Dinny is upon them raving:

"What—Maher? Where are the horses?"

    "Here! Sir What's the matter? Are they after us?" "They are! they are! O
blessed night! I'm burning!"

    "Who are they?"

"All that's evil, I think! Mount and be off—Don't you see 'em—and hear
'em—and feel 'em? *I* do, if you don't—There—there?" he added, dashing
the chalice at Maher's feet. . . . (*T*, 413)

Mun's mother curses Dinny for his deed, and the madman rushes at her about to strangle her when he believes the fires of hell are suddenly about him. The fires of St. John's Eve are being lighted at that moment while the mountains and plains glow red with the evening sun.

Approaching those fires very rapidly is Byrne's party, and among them Robert Kumba. Just as the past and present are a part of Dinny's sacrilegious act so also are they one in Kumba's thoughts. He regrets deeply all he has done to destroy his chances for happiness. While his misery has grown in dissipation, Lilly has found solace in obeying her father. She has been made morally stronger and wiser in the ordeal of giving up Kumba.

As the narrator completes his thematic, reinforcing series of flashbacks into the lives of his principal characters—Dinny, Sally, and her father—he now prepares the Byrnes' home in Drumscanlon for Lilly's attempted abduction by Dinny. Lilly has just finished singing some lyrics Kumba used to sing to her, and the words reassure her that the adjustment she has made at her father's request is responsible for her present control and self-possession. Lightning suddenly appears in the sky, the lights abruptly go out in the house, and Lilly disappears in search of candles. James Mihil, a servant, has just finished lighting St. John's fires, thereby linking the chapel scene with what is about to happen at Drumscanlon. Awney Farrel, Maney MacO'Neil and others of the band arrive moments later and seize Mihil. When Dinny tries to ride off with Lilly, Kumba dashes in only to be stopped by a bullet from Dinny's pistol. Facing Segur at last, the "coiner" laughs at the old man's command to release the girl and to surrender. Griffin gives each his say about the injuries that have flowed between them before Segur finally shoots Dinny when he attempts to escape. The review of both men's past lives, melodramatically delivered before the fatal shot, checks the tendency on the part of Griffin's readers to be attracted to Dinny's outlaw figure (or so the author hopes). Moreover, old Segur's role of judge and executioner seems less justified now. The total absence of legal authority permeates the entire scene.

The tale closes upon the note that Kumba recovers not only from his wound but from the effects of his years of dissipation. His reputation is restored and Lilly is now free to marry him. Regretting deeply that greed which prompted him to leave his daughter in the first place, Segur returns with Sally to his native land. Sally lives to erase all traces of her disobedience and selfishness.

Through the physical and psychological converging of time and space in the actions and thoughts of his characters, Griffin structures

the events of his tale of the return of exiles to justice and peace. Dinny's
conscience, for example, is stirred by his sacrilegious acts in the church,
and here Griffin accounts for superstition in terms of his "obstinate
resistance to the truth of religion." Kumba's conscience is regenerated,
but here a distinction must be made. From birth Dinny was a victim
of his country's history, right up to the end when he is executed by a
foreigner, Issac Segur.

Griffin's attempt to fuse dramatically the regeneration of a middleman and the punishment of a peasant outlaw is realized in the structure of events which culminate at the home of Lilly Byrne. She has
been throughout the story the single example of chastity and obedience, and just as Dinny desecrated the host, in the church, so he seems
bent on Lilly's destruction. Kumba knows her influence for good.

Griffin's art and preachment in this tale include not only thematic
structuring of scenes but thematic imagery as well. The contrasting
weather that accompanies Dinny's band and Cuthbert's party rein-
forces Griffin's moral structure: Kumba is chastened not only by his
remembrance of his past deeds but by the storm through which he
moves. Dinny is reminded of the good things of his past life by the
beauties of nature he is viewing for the last time on St. John's Eve.

Griffin chose religious festivals as the occasions for setting the foibles
of his Munstermen before his readers because religious holidays meant
religious instruction. In the return of his exiles, whether they are exiles
from their native land or from their parents, chastened hearts make
good adjustments which contribute to the peace and unity of a
community.

The order of the *Tales* seems to suggest the growth of Griffin's powers as a novelist. The actions of characters like Duke Dorgan in "Card
Drawing" are described—he does very little acting. Eugene Hamond
is more fully realized—he speaks and acts forcefully. His inner
thoughts deepen the significance of his performance. Griffin lost some
of his diffidence as a writer when he began to allow his own experiences to become part of his writing. For example, Hamond's reactions
to Emily's Dublin circle, the Anglo-Irish aristocracy, were also Griffin's, on those occasions when he too found himself in unfamiliar company. "Suil Dhuv," Griffin's best piece in the series, shows his talent
for arranging scenes and juxtaposing characters for maximum exposure. A slackening in the application of melodrama, Griffin's principal
weakness, is also apparent in "Suil Dhuv." Pryce Kinchela's remorse,
arrived at while he hangs over a cliff's edge at the end of a rope, is far

less effective than the chapel scene in which Dinny's past becomes his present and his tortured soul is bared.

Implied Christian principles of education and psychological insight into human motivations and actions were now two of Griffin's most important subjects. He was a teacher in his art and an artist in his teaching. He was an artist of feelings and the times in which they occurred. He knew how to portray the dignity and failure of his people. The misfits of his stories appear as strong deterrents to the peace and unity of his nation for which he daily prayed. The success of *The Collegians*, however, irrevocably changed the direction his art was taking in the *Tales*.

CHAPTER 5

The Collegians

GERALD Griffin spent approximately eight months trying to find a subject for his next book. The faults found in the *Tales* by the reviewers, he admitted, were caused by "over eagerness and precipitancy,"[1] but his extreme sensitivity in the face of any criticism, at this time, did not permit him to begin a new book immediately. The *Tales* were to have settled the matter of his remaining a writer or not, and the results were tantalizing: the critics were justified in their slight faultfinding, and the public was delighted by the stories. Consequently, desperation, ambition, and passion went into the selection of an actual crime as his next subject. He courted realism, "this rage of the day," more than ever before, and for the first time in his career he entered the souls of the characters he was creating, but not without feeling remorse for having done so. Nevertheless, he wrote with no more deliberation than he had ever expended. This time writing became a "recollected truth."

His subject was romance and murder, and for his source he did what Scott had done for his story of *The Heart of Midlothian*. Scott had received an account of one Helen Walker who obtained a pardon for her sister's crime from the duke of Argyle after having walked from Scotland to London to accomplish it.[2] No less celebrated an event in Munster in the year 1819 was the trial of John Scanlon for the murder of his wife Ellen Hanley, and ten years later Griffin was to follow closely in his fiction many of the facts of this crime he had learned as a boy of fifteen.

Griffin took John Scanlon, Ellen Hanley, and Stephen Sullivan, the actual assassin, and created Hardress Cregan, Eily O'Connor, and Danny ("the Lord") Mann. His passion to succeed produced one effortless flow of creativity. He recalled the facts of the crime and added his own fictional details in a characteristically didactic fashion. The old themes are here, but Griffin was putting himself into this writing as he had never done before (or was ever to do again). Hardress Cregan and

Kyrle Daly are Griffin's voices—private and public—debating his future as an artist just as Cregan and Daly debate the values implicit in being true to nature or in being conventional and hence affected. Cregan's argument against "giving the mind an unwholesome preponderance over the heart"[3] is romantic and naive. Cregan is Griffin's most successful creation, yet he became a spiritual threat to the man who had to shun passion in his life and in his art. Kyrle Daly's reason and calm win out prosaically in a book never wholly given over to the artist's talents.

I   The Collegians: *Summary and Analysis*

As a work of art, *The Collegians* ranks with the best by such contemporary Irish writers as Maria Edgeworth and John Banim. The work of the greatest English novelist of Griffin's day, Sir Walter Scott, casts *The Collegians* in favorable light when, for example, Madge Wildfire is compared to Poll Naughten. However, before *The Collegians* is compared to the works of these and other English and Irish novelists of both the eighteenth and nineteenth centuries, there should follow a sketch of the plot of Griffin's finest work.

In the opening scene, the village of Garryowen is alive to the news of Eily O'Connor's disappearance. Before she reappears as the wife of Hardress Cregan, Munster life in the late eighteenth century begins to unfold. Kyrle Daly, a middleman, sets off to woo Anne Chute, a local aristocratic beauty. As he travels the road to Castle Chute and his disappointment, he is accompanied by his peasant friend Lowry Looby, who entertains him with anecdotes and songs. Arriving at Castle Chute, Kyrle finds Myles-na-Coppaleen, a mountaineer, answering charges that his wild ponies have trespassed on the Chutes' property. He demolishes the accusation with the quick wit of the peasants who have learned to endure the worst of the Penal days and are experiencing now some semblance of economic independence.

With his brief introduction to the Dalys, the Chutes, Looby, and Myles, Griffin has presented three classes of Munster provincial society quite distinct yet beginning to merge through social, political, and economic forces which they themselves are sponsoring and opposing at the same time. The Dalys are the middlemen who are slowly rising on the socioeconomic plane, but not so rapidly that Mr. Daly would encourage his son to court the daughter of his social and economic superior. In the scene with the Chutes, who with the Cregans constitute the gentry, and Myles, Griffin points to the past and the present marking the time when the peasant began to demand his natural rights and the moment about to arrive when he and the Catholic Association under the leadership of Daniel O'Connell would defy the British government in order to be heard on the matter of basic freedoms.

The first meeting between Cregan and Daly, both graduates of Trinity College, Dublin, reveals the contrasting natures of these two men who are soon to have one matter in common—their love for Anne Chute. It is Daly who provokes Cregan by praising the refinement and education Anne possesses. "She is cold and distant," remarks Cregan, "even to absolute frigidity, merely because she has been taught that insensibility is allied to elegance" (C, 121). When he declaims the beauty of living one with nature in all her magnitude and simplicity, he is speaking, he believes, with certitude and knowledge. He sails, for example, with incomparable skill and abandon. The irony of his denunciation of Miss Chute lies in the fact that he does not know how he will react to polite society, nor can he possibly suspect Miss Chute is soon to charm him completely.

Cregan's mother is anxious for her son to meet Anne and arranges for their introduction at a ball. Hardress finds himself being drawn to Anne, and the shock of such an awareness causes him to behave in ways as incomprehensible to himself as they are to others about him, particularly to his mother. Mrs. Cregan, unaware of Hardress's marriage to Eily O'Connor, urges her son to marry the wealthy and beautiful heiress. Cregan's dilemma is resolved finally when his follower, Danny Mann, murders Eily. Soon after the murder Cregan is apprehended by the law as he hides in his mother's bedroom. While Kyrle is left with some hope that he will eventually win Anne's love, Cregan suffers death in exile, and Danny's life ends in agony of remorse.

Griffin's characters in *The Collegians* are far superior to those of his earlier works. They are fully motivated figures who react to the new information which they daily encounter. However, as artistically finished as the entire book seems in its characterizations, setting, and plot, as knowledgeable as Griffin's sociological approach to this eighteenth-century Irish scene appears, the precisely balanced structure of characters and scenes produces a moral impact indicative of the fact that teaching a moral lesson in literature was inevitable for Griffin, even when he seemed most unfettered by his scruples. The moral structure of *The Collegians*, the form its movements and parts take in delivering his preachments, mark his finest artistic effort and signal the end of his artistic growth.

Griffin referred to *The Collegians* as a "domestic drama," and having used all his powers as a dramatist he structured his scenes to advance a Roman Catholic theme of duty to God and to family. He was certainly intent upon achieving a balance in the emotional response of his readers. Tension caused by the conflict which Hardress creates is evenly distributed through a logical and unified series of scenes patterning the emotions of Griffin's characters and directing the reactions and emotions of his readers. The entire structure of *The Collegians* consists of precise juxtaposings of characters and scenes for a moral impact. As Lowry Looby and Danny Mann parody Hardress Cregan and Kyrle Daly, for example, or Cregan contrasts Daly, the reader encounters "a social novel, embracing all classes and conditions"[4] and is directed along the moral plane of duty to God and family.

The Collegians begins with two movements: Kyrle Daly's venture to Castle Chute to woo Anne Chute and Hardress Cregan's and Eily O'Connor's flight to get married. In the former movement the reader is treated to the superb characterization of Lowry Looby whose peasant charm, wit, and uproarious appearance parallel and parody Daly's quest of Miss Chute. Middleman Daly's confusion and doubt as he approaches the castle is contrasted by Looby's songs, anecdotes, and play with a pretty peasant girl whom he meets along the way.

Hardress's and Eily's flight comprises the beginning of all the trouble that Cregan is to bring upon himself: he, a member of the gentry, is marrying the beautiful peasant girl Eily O'Connor, daughter of Mihil O'Connor "who conducted the business of a rope-walk in the neighborhood of Garryowen" (*C,* 7). Griffin is quick to point to the beautiful Eily's "brash and vulgar education" in the suspenseful buildup of the lovers' flight upon the river which is first viewed by the Dalys from their breakfast window and later observed by Kyrle and Looby on their way to Castle Chute. No other scene in the book places Cregan in a more advantageous light as the bold, romantic hero than the flight scene in which he defies the forces of nature with skill and daring. And when Cregan and Daly finally meet in a cottage during the storm and after Cregan marries Eily, the terrible irony of the novel appears in the words of Daly who defends education and refinement against Cregan's romantic cry for heart over reason, nature over affectation: "It would be too late, after you had linked yourself to-to-simplicity, I shall call it, to discover that elegance was a good thing after all" (*C,* 125).

As Hardress moves to his union with the ropemaker's daughter, Kyrle proposes to the aristocratic Anne only to be disappointed. At this point Griffin fixes the two paths the collegians are to travel: Kyrle, the middleman, accepts his setback, reaffirms his belief in control through reason, but he is in no way able to put Anne out of his mind: "The love which Kyrle entertained for this lady was so singular, so rational, and regulated by so fine a principle of judgment, that the warmest, the wisest, and the best of men might condescend to take an interest in its success" (C, 58). Ironically, it is Cregan who promises to speak for his friend during the interval that Anne is to stay with the Cregans and who turns from his peasant bride once he discovers his potential for social success and his place in Anne's heart. The irony of his vehement defense of simplicity in all things is deepened further in terms of his part in Eily's destruction and his disastrous relationship with Anne Chute, now being urged upon him more than ever by his mother after he begins to collapse under the strain of his involvement in Eily's death.

Knowing that the Irish peasantry are "more distinguished for quick and kindly feeling than for a just perception of moral excellence" (C, 59), Griffin presents Danny Mann as Cregan's faithful retainer and stages the dramatic temptation scene: standing upon a mountaintop enveloped in mist, Cregan is tempted by Danny the Lord. The nature imagery; the ironic, philosophic remarks of Danny on permanence and change; Cregan's half-conscious acceptance of Danny's suggestions that Eily be eliminated, and hence the lack of full consent of the will, impress the reader with the effects of Danny's unreasoning and blind loyalty and show Hardress as every bit "his mother's spoiled pet, nursed in the very lap of passion, and ruined by indulgence."[5] The culminating scene of Cregan's misadventure appropriately takes place in Mrs. Cregan's bedroom where Hardress is found hiding from the authorities.

The fates of the two collegians, Cregan's exile and death and Kyrle's final success with the chastened Anne, are amplified by the other richly dramatic, highly didactic, warmly humorous scenes involving the inheritors of Munster culture, Griffin's peasants, who possess grace, wit, and pathos. They move parallel much of the time to the fortunes of the collegians, offering objectivity, irony, and common sense compounded by a remembrance of things past and a glowing pride in their ability to endure.

There is no mistaking the effect that Myles Murphy has upon the gentry of Castle Chute. His personal appearance and his facility of speech and wit, characteristic of his class, are given a fine showing by the author. He completely captivates gentry and garrison and successfully carries his plea. Lowry Looby's riotous performance in the "stag-geen race," superbly recorded in the reactions of Anne, Kyrle, and Captain Gibson of the garrison, is even more appealing since it relieves the reader of the tedium of Kyrle's pursuit of Anne, which is faltering badly at this stage. Danny Mann's being "pinked" by Hyland Creagh, "a squireen," is as pathetic as Dalton's death in the service of the drunken master of "Roaring Hall."

When Kyrle and Hardress part after their first meeting and discussion of simplicity versus affectation, Griffin presents Lowry and Danny upon the same subject; their peasant humor tends to lighten the somber moral tone set by the collegians, thus allowing Griffin to make his point again and more directly to another audience. Looby begins: "'Unless he could smoke two pipes of a night, instead of one, or sleep more, or ate more without hurt, I don't say what's the advantage a king has over a poor man like myself.' 'Ah, sure, you know that's foolish talk, Lowry. Sure the king could buy and sell you at the fair if he loiked.' 'He couldn't without the jury,' returned Lowry—'the judge an' jury ever. He couldn't lay a wet finger or me without the jury, be course o' law. The round o' the world is as free to me as it is to him, if the world be round in airnest, as they say it is'" (*C*, 132).

Captain Gibson's words regarding the Irish peasant are profoundly true, for the art of living, in this sense surviving, precludes cooperation with British authority in Ireland, and Griffin's profoundest irony, as the writer of *The Collegians*, lies in the fact that his peasant creatures appear most real because their models were natural actors. When Danny the Lord appears before Magistrate Warner after his arrest for the murder of Eily, he speaks for generations of Irishmen: "I knew your laws of old. It isn't for noting that we see de fathers of families, de pride an' de strength of our villages, de young an' de old, de guilty an' de innocent, snatched away from their own cabins, an' shared off for transportation an' de gallows. It isn't for noting our brothers, our cousins, an' our friends are hanged before our doores from year to year. Dey taich us something of de law, we tank 'em" (*C*, 404). The law taught the meaning of the class system, maintained the separation of the classes, and thus necessitated everyone to become actors to support a daily, social intercourse between a superficial gentry and a fiercely determined brotherhood.

Poll Naughten's devastating satire of Hardress proceeds from whiskey, but she knows exactly what he is about with his courting of Anne Chute and secretly keeping Eily at the Naughtens' hovel. She is a match for Cregan's class and is no less effective against the magistrate,

Mr. Warner, who is unable to wring information from her concerning Eily's letter sent to her father before his death. Captain Gibson, "purple from suppressed laughter" at Poll's performance, can only order the amazon's being remanded. Equally effective against the law is Phil Naughten, who, when questioned on the same matter, answers in Irish.

As morally instructive as Cregan's character and fate seem to be, so also is the love and determination of those who follow him. Danny Mann would kill for his master; Eily would die for her husband. When Cregan shut her up with the Naughtens immediately following their flight and marriage, Eily became desperate and fled to her uncle, Father Edward in Castle Island. By offering Eily a "double" in the mountain girl who directs her to her uncle, Griffin compounds Eily's anguish and hence its moral force. As Eily's guide tells her story of disobedience to her father, the reader is given the opportunity of creating the anguish that Eily is undoubtedly experiencing, for Griffin offers no trace of the torture Eily is enduring. Particularly effective for its moral force is Eily's decision, after hearing the mountain girl's story which parallels her own and after being admonished by Father Edward, to return to the Naughtens and to meet her death. She is deceived in her love, which admits no guidance from reason.

The "squireens" have their code and it is as comic and pathetic in some aspects as that of the peasants. Mr. Cregan's involvement with his cronies, Hepton Connolly and Hyland "Fire-ball" Creagh, has left Hardress to the almost exclusive influence of his mother. However, Hardress is still able to learn from his father's friends what no classroom experience at Trinity could teach him. When Hardress disdains the practice of dueling and swears he could never fight a duel, it is but moments before Creagh draws him into a match and gleefully spares him. Cregan is "not of age," and the rashness of his words before the experienced hand of Creagh serves to enlarge upon the image of the young romantic who proposes marriage to the sixteen-year-old daughter of a ropemaker.

Cregan's father is not without his "follower." He has been blessed with the service and devotion of Dalton, his old huntsman, who now lies dying as his master lies prostrate from drink. Old Dalton on his deathbed is called upon for one last "fox-huntin' screech" before he dies. Ironically, it is Cregan senior who has given up foxhunting for cockfighting, but in the last moments of Dalton's life, Cregan calls for this last gesture to conclude the evening's entertainment of giving accounts of cockfights and ghosts. Griffin juxtaposes the two men, the one crawling nearly "dead drunk" across the hall's floor and the other dying in the room below, to point to the extreme but believable view of the two classes—the one intent upon possessing the other; that other helpless but grand in the cruel service. The comic and the pathetic are closely allied in this scene, as they are in others, to allow Griffin's heavy moral tone of duty to God and family to permeate the entire tale. Similarly, as the scenes involving dissolution in the lives of the Cregans impress the reader, so also do the few involving the Dalys offer what life among aspiring middle-class men is like.

Griffin, with all of the dramatist's bent on holding his audience, carefully allots sufficient space to advance the Dalys' high moral character. He knows they are dull and sentimental in comparison to the Cregans and hence less entertaining. However, it is Griffin's profound respect for Christian principles in the home that prompts this contrast to the Cregans: he remembers, in his art, life at Fairy Lawn before his mother and father, Ellen and Patrick, sailed for America.

The opening domestic scene of the Dalys at breakfast, characterized by family love, comfort, and conviviality, receives its contrast in the dramatization of Mrs. Daly's death in childbirth. Yet, from this latest ordeal Kyrle emerges with "a higher feeling of duty." His initial disappointment in his proposal to Anne, the betrayal of his friend Cregan, and now his mother's death prepare him for life in a way that Cregan could never understand. The pressure from his mother to marry Anne and his unconfessed guilt nearly derange him. Although Hardress's figure was far more pleasing to the reading public, that of Kyrle Daly was a great consolation to an artist who was opposing the dictates of his deepest religious feelings as he wrote his best book.

II *Griffin and His Masters*

As Griffin created his masterpiece, he discovered what he had to be. His psychological makeup made him feel deeply the artist's dilemma of trying to settle upon himself the laurels which he believed his talent deserved and eschewing the very means by which he was able to succeed—writing about human passions. Hardress Cregan and Kyrle Daly are extensions of Griffin's ambivalent feelings about life and art. His passion for success was checked by scrupulosity, pride, and diffidence to the point that he finally abandoned art for a monastic life, but not before he recorded his conflict in *The Collegians*. Aubrey De Vere and everyone who read *The Collegians* expected "a long series of historic romances illustrating Ireland as Scott's had illustrated Scotland."[6] Griffin had the talent to continue in the popular vein of *The Collegians*, but he chose not to do so. He left only one book worthy of comparison to his English and Anglo-Irish masters in the dramatic and moral tradition of the novel. Let it suffice in this writing to juxtapose characters from Griffin's masterpiece with those of writers like Fielding, Edgeworth, Scott, and Banim in order to comment on the probable influence their work produced in his writing and to suggest more comprehensively the merits of one of Ireland's first novelists.

When Griffin condemned Fielding for his "grossly licentious works,"[7] he was reacting to Tom and Mrs. Waters or Tom and Lady Bellaston; for the moment he forgot the highly didactic *Amelia*. Eily O'Connor's faith in divine providence is akin to Amelia's, and her loyalty to Hardress is matched by that shown to Captain Booth by his own faithful and long-suffering wife. Fielding's un-Christian, lawless London scene enables his characters to prove their worth to one another just as Griffin's lawless, Munster milieu frames his people's actions.

To Mr. Bondum, Captain Booth's bailiff, liberty means having sufficient funds to remain free. Any other meaning is incomprehensible to him: "Booth desired the bailiff to give him his opinion on liberty. Upon which, he hesitated a moment, and then cried out, 'Oh, 'tis a fine thing, 'tis a very fine thing, and the constitution of England.' Booth told him, that by the old constitution of England he had heard that men could not be arrested for debt; to which the bailiff answered, that must have been in very bad times. . . ."[8] As impotent as Booth's position appears before the face of law and imprisonment, so also does Cregan's ineffectual response to a tenant's story stand:

"Well, the sarvant boy comes in, as it might be to my cabin there (if he had anything again me) and without ever saying one word, he walks in to the middle o' the floore, an' lays the whip-handle upon the table, and walks out again without ever saying one word. . . . Well, up they go to the great house, an' there they ax for the masther, an' they carry the whip-handle into his parlour, where he locks the door upon 'em, an' if they can't well account for what they done, he makes 'em sthrip, and begins flaking 'em with a horse-whip until their backs is all one grishkin; an' then he tells 'em to go about their business, an' let him hear no more complaints in the future. I thought it was a ghost I seen myself, last night, when I found the whip-handle on my own table. But I made all clear when I seen the masther."

"That is pushing his authority to a feudal extent," said Hardress.

"A what, sir?" asked Phil, looking puzzled.

"Nothing, Phil, nothing." (*C*, 188)

In both instances, absence of the law means brutalization of the poor. In both books, the message is for reform and the art in telling it is quite instructive: the status quo aborts justice through misconception and inhumanity.

No less an educator in her prose is Maria Edgeworth, whose outstanding work, *Castle Rackrent*, serves not only to enlighten an English world about the nature of its sister isle but to inspire such artists as Banim, Griffin, and Carleton to treat the matter of Ireland. Thady Quirk is Miss Edgeworth's finest peasant creation, and his service to her as an ingenious interlocutor for the masters of Castle Rackrent is superbly performed.

Upon the occasion of Sir Condy's election to Parliament, Thady's master has eliminated a menacing creditor, and the old retainer is delighted:

"Is that Sir Condy Rackrent in the chair?" says a stranger man in the crowd.

"The same," says I. "Who else could it be? God bless him!"

"And I take it, then, you belong to him?" says he.

"Not at all," says I; "but I live under him, and have done so these two hundred years and upwards, me and mine."

"It's lucky for you, then," rejoins he, "that he is where he is; for was he anywhere else but in the chair, this minute he'd be in a worse place; for I was sent down on purpose to put him up, and here's my order for so doing in my pocket." . . .

"Put it in your pocket again, and think no more of it anyways for seven years to come, my honest friend," says I; "he's a member of Parliament now, praised be God. . . ."⁹

Thady appears so real because he is based on John Langan, steward to Richard Lovell Edgeworth, Maria's father. With the success of Thady Quirk's performance, Griffin did not hesitate to conjure the wit and charm of the Munster peasant as the following scene from *The Collegians* demonstrates: Lowry Looby is at Kyrle Daly's side as the two make their way to Castle Chute in the opening pages of *The Collegians*:

"Lowry!" shouted Kyrle Daly.

"Going, sir!"

"Going? I think you *are* going, and at a pretty brisk rate, too. You travel merrily, Lowry."

"Middlin', sir, middlin'—as the world goes. I sing for company, ever and always, when I go a long road by myself, an' I find it a dale pleasanter and lighter on me. Equal to the lark, that the louder he sings the higher he mounts, it's the way with me, an' I travellin'—the lighter my heart the faster the road slips from under me." (C, 44)

Griffin's potential subjects were known to flee his company, once they became aware of his identity, in fear of becoming one of his "crathurs."

The more somber tones of peasant life in Griffin's neighborhood are sounded by characters like Danny Mann and Poll Naughten who oppose successfully the machinery of British law through daring and subtlety practiced against the oppressor for centuries. Poll baffles the magistrate who questions her concerning Eily O'Connor's disappearance:

"Hear me, my good woman. If you won't speak out, we shall find a way to make you speak."

"No use in wasting blows upon a willing horse: I can do no more than speak to the best of my ability."

"Very well. I ask you again, therefore, whether Looby received a letter from you on that evening?"

"Does Lowry say I gev him a letther?"

"You will not answer, then?"

"To be sure I will. What am I here for?"

"To drive me mad, I believe."

"Faix, I can't help you," said Poll, "when you won't listen to me."

"Well, well, speak on."

"I will, then, without a word of a lie. I'll tell you the whole business, and let Lowry himself conthradict me if he daar to do it. 'Tis as good as six years ago, now, since I met that boy at one o' the Hewsan's wakes."

"Well, what has that to do with an answer to a plain question?"

"Easy a minute, can't you, an' I'll tell you. He behaved very polished that night, an' I seen no more of him until the day you spake of, when he came into the cottage from Killarney."

"Woman," said the magistrate, "remember that you have sworn to tell the whole truth; not only the truth, but the whole truth."

"Ah, then, gentleman an' lady, d'ye hear this? Did anybody ever hear the peer o' that? Sure it's just the whole truth I'm tellin' him, an' he won't listen to half of it."

"Go on," said Mr. Warner, in a tone of resignation.

"Sure, that's what I want to do, if I'd be let. I say this, an' I'll stand to it. Lowry gave me impidence that I wouldn't stand from his masther, an' I did (let him make the most of it) I admit it, I did give him a sthroke or two. I did. I admit it."

"And after the *sthrokes,* as you call them, you gave him a letter?"

"What letther?"

"I see; you are very copious in your admissions. Are you Philip Naughten's wife?"

"I am."

"Ay, now we're upon smooth ground. You can give an answer when it suits you. I'm afraid you are too many for me. What shall we do with this communicative person?" he said, turning to the other gentlemen.

"Remand her," said Captain Gibson, whose face was purple from suppressed laughter. . . . (*C,* 378–79)

As wily as Poll is upon this occasion, Madge Wildfire, in Sir Walter Scott's *The Heart of Midlothian,* is no less quick-witted when questioned by Jeanie about her sister's baby:

"Aha, lass,—catch me if you can—I think it's easy to gar you trow onything.—How suld I ken onything o' your sister's wean? Lasses suld hae naething to do wi' weans till they are married—and then a' the gossips and cummers come in and feast as if it were the blithest day in the warld.—They say maidens' bairns are well guided. I wot that wasna true of your tittie's and mine; but these are sad tales to tell."[10]

As a very young man Griffin thought of surpassing Scott but soon found the task insurmountable. Occasionally, however, his creations, like Poll Naughten and Lowry Looby, appear as authentic fixtures in a region and a period which Griffin faithfully represented to his readers for the first time.

"Crohoore of the Bill-Hook" from *Tales of the O'Hara Family* by John Banim undoubtedly impressed Griffin who knew that his friend wrote of firsthand experience, in this instance the work of the Leinster "Whiteboys." As an example of why these men took oaths to revenge themselves upon their oppressors—be they magistrates, soldiers, bailiffs, tithe-proctors, ministers, or priests—Banim has his hero Pierce Shea view a victim of the brutal Protestant tithe system on the night Pierce appears before them desperately seeking his abducted lover, Alley Dooling:

Pierce turned towards the place: there was no fire on the hearth; but upon the hob, and deeply shaded by the projection of the huge chimney, sat a man about forty, without shoes, stockings, coat, or vest; a small-clothes and soot-stained shirt his only covering. His arms were folded hard, his chin sunk into his breast, his bare legs crossed, and he swung and jogged them to and fro, in action that betokened a sullen and desperate indifference to the ruin about him.

"Ay, there they is, now," he continued, as Pierce stared at him in silence: "one, two, three o' them; an' I'm their father, an' what am I to do wid 'em?"

"Where's their mother?" asked Pierce.

"Avoch, an' what a question you put on me; I went down the bosheen, yesterday, after the proctor left us, an' I tould 'em she was gaspin'; yes, I tould 'em my wife was gaspin', an' the good christhens wouldn't believe me; an' yet she was stiff afore me when I cum back, an' I buried her widout a wake, or a sheet, to wind her in. . . ."[11]

Pierce continues to look about the cabin:

Close by one wall, ran a rough deal plank, supported by piles of loose stones, forming the seat upon which, at a narrow table, about a dozen men were crowded; and at its other side, large stones, without any plank or board, supplied seats to some half dozen more. There was no chimney; but two benches, built of slate and clay, enclosed an area, within which a few sods of turf emitted a feeble blaze; and sitting very near, crippled up into a lump, her knees reaching higher than her head, her bleared eyes steadfastly fixed on the decaying embers, and her whole air and position shewing an uncon-sciousness or carelessness of the dinning noise, was the hostess of this lowly *auberge*. In the corner to her left appeared an enclosure of rough stones that fenced in the heath on which she lay; and in the other, a roughly-constructed and uncouthly-shaped barrel, from which, by the agency of spigot and fauset, she drew, in wooden noggins, and as her guests claimed it, the stout though now exploded shebeen.[12]

These men are as desperate in their business as Pierce is in his quest. When one of them, the schoolmaster, explains the "Whiteboys'" mis-sion in the neighborhood, Banim steps in to speak for his hero Pierce Shea: "'but my father has all along taught me to ask what I now ask you—how much good has come or can come from all you are able to do? little mischief to your real oppressors, and your own death upon the gallows more certainly than the relief you look for.'"[13] Pierce's words mean nothing to these men whose hearts are broken and whose determination for revenge is unshakable. He soon begins to drink and to sympathize with their cause, having never before experienced such misery. The following evening he rides out with the gang and witnesses the mutilation of Peery Clancy, the tithe-proctor. Griffin joined Banim in the theme of education: both felt that with the young there was hope for a peaceful future.

Banim exerted the profoundest influence on Gerald Griffin, who saw clearly the importance of his friend's faithful recording: the matter of Leinster would now be joined by that of Munster and the two regions of Ireland opened their store of storm and travail to men of peace and dedication.

Implied or explicitly stated, the theme of education is part of the actions of characters like Cregan or Pierce Shea. Authors like Fielding and Griffin make their point about the purpose of art for life. Fielding writes that "by observing minutely the several incidents which tend to the catastrophe or completion of the whole, and the minute causes whence those incidents are produced, we shall best be instructed in this most useful of all arts, which I call the Art of Life."[14] Griffin closes *The Collegians* with similar sentiments: "Reader, if you have shuddered at the excesses into which he [Cregan] plunged, examine your own heart, and see if it hide nothing of the intellectual pride and volatile susceptibility of new impressions, which were the ruin of Hardress Cregan. If, besides the amusement which these pages may have afforded, you should learn anything from such research for the avoidance of evil, or the pursuit of good, it will not be in vain that we have penned the story of our two COLLEGIANS" (*C*, 437).

The matter of Gaelic Ireland in the nineteenth century is still an impressive subject to the children of Clare or to Limerick farmers who today speak familiarly about *The Collegians*. Griffin's best work is alive in the tradition of imparting Christian principles for the education of the young of Ireland. He wrote one very good novel and represented some of the best efforts of Ireland's first novelists.

CHAPTER 6

Moral Eclipse

*T*ALES *of the Munster Festivals: The Rivals and Tracy's Ambition* (1830), *The Christian Physiologist* (1830), and *The Invasion* (1832) clearly indicate that Griffin abandoned the formula he had discovered in writing *The Collegians.* His writing was now a part of his daily prayers for guidance into a religious life, and from his experience with *The Collegians* he was acutely aware of the fact that one element in a book or story could completely set aside the moral purpose he had in mind for his reader. The balance of psychological realism in "Tracy's Ambition" and the dense moral tone of "The Rivals" attest to the fact that Griffin's scrupulosity would never again allow his readers to be merely entertained.

The Christian Physiologist, written during the opening year of Griffin's relationship with Lydia Fisher, is a collection of moral tales for children. To some extent, the work he was doing among the poor children of Pallas Kenry, in addition to his pleasurable task of tutoring one of Lydia's children, prompted him to compile such a book. Authors before him had written instructional material for children; for example, Maria Edgeworth's *Moral Tales for Young People* (1801) manifests her interest in the kind of education Griffin was to assume as a Christian Brother in 1838. The fact that *The Christian Physiologist* was published so soon after his meeting Lydia suggests the impact that fervent Quaker had upon the young celebrity. As his most influential critic and advisor and the woman he so hopelessly loved, Lydia Fisher was the most deciding factor in Gerald's decision to enter a monastery. *The Christian Physiologist* is a reflection of the emotional tension the young author was attempting to cast off. Frustrated by the uncertainty of his career, particularly after his success with *The Collegians,* and now in love with a married woman, he set to writing a book about how good Christians are to regulate their senses for God's greater glory and their own salvation.

Research for *The Invasion* began immediately following the publication of *The Collegians* in 1829. Griffin believed that there were "many peculiarities in the images of early times which would admit of being blended with a story, and would keep up that interest in the public mind, about the decline of which he was always apprehensive."[1] Enthused with his idea he proceeded to libraries in London and Dublin, and it was during his Dublin researches that he paused to be toasted by Sir Philip Crampton, the surgeon general, and by the literary circle of that great city. Having turned to such a subject as ancient Ireland, Griffin believed he was being of service to his people and drawing himself closer to service to God.

Griffin had listened always to two voices, but during the years 1828 through 1830, his private voice was gaining full sway, and in these two books, *Tales of the Munster Festivals: The Rivals and Tracy's Ambition* and *The Invasion*, its influence can be traced as success became moral paralysis.

I *"The Rivals"*

The predominant tone of "The Rivals," one that Griffin described as "religious sadness," rises from the locale of Glendalough in the Wicklow Mountains of County Wicklow, in eastern and central Ireland. Legend and history combine today as in Griffin's time: he viewed the magnificent round tower 105 feet high with a 48-foot base used to protect the inhabitants against the Norse marauders; St. Kevin's Cross, an eleven foot granite monolith; the oratory of St. Kevin's Kitchen; and of special interest to the novelist and poet, St. Kevin's Bed, a rock ledge high atop the cliffs which surrounded the entire area and from which, according to legend, the saint pushed the infatuated Cathleen to her death in the lake below. Griffin based his poem "The Fate of Cathleen" on the legend and sent it to Lydia Fisher, having felt, perhaps, somewhat akin to the good saint of the legend. This gentle admonition to Lydia echoes in his refusal to see her upon her visitation to the Christian Brothers' monastery in Dublin. He was beginning his service to God, and apparently such an encounter would have been unwise.

Resurrection is the principal theme in "The Rivals," the first of the two tales comprising *Tales of the Munster Festivals*, third series, published in 1830. As melodramatic and redundant as scenes from "The Rivals" become with their religious and political overtones, the tale displays Griffin as a master storyteller of his people and their times.

II "*The Rivals*": Summary and Analysis

Richard Lacy and Francis Riordan, members of the Protestant
Ascendancy, quarrel over the affections of Esther Wilderming, a ward
of Mr. Kirwan Damer, and Lacy is wounded. Riordan then leaves the
country with other Irish patriots to fight with Bolivar in South America.
As the story begins, Esther is about to sign the marriage agreement
preparatory to marrying Richard Lacy. At this point Griffin commences his theme of resurrection: Esther is startled by what she
believes to be Riordan's words of warning against the engagement.
Nevertheless, the affair is settled and the villainous Lacy is soon to wed
Esther.

Griffin's rivals are not limited to Esther's suitors. Mr. Damer, a
wealthy magistrate and a self-proclaimed benefactor of the Irish Catholic peasant, is opposed by a less enlightened magistrate, Tom Leonard.
Mr. Aaron Shepher, Damer's Methodist servant, is Davy Lenigan's
rival in the matter of salvation: the Methodist way versus the Roman
Catholic prescription. Rivals or contrasting characters, these creations
of Griffin bear the identical message throughout the melodrama and
comedy—tolerance and charity mean peace and happiness.

Upon his return from Colombia, Riordan learns of Esther's death on
the eve of her wedding. Heartbroken, he proceeds with Davy to
Esther's tomb for one last look at his loved one. Once inside the vault,
Riordan imagines he hears Esther's voice. Disregarding Davy's objec-
tions about opening the coffin, he tears off the lid and views Esther's
beautiful remains. Not content with her present resting place, he carries the body to a nearby cottage for burial at the place where they
met as lovers. Once at the cottage, Esther returns to consciousness
"completely recovered from the effect of that paroxysm of her neur-
algic illness which has for so long a time left her in a trance resembling
death, and had maintained the latent principle of existence for so many
hours even in her coffin" (Davy counts three days!) (*T*, 97). Joyfully
reunited, the couple marry and go to live by a lovely little lake in the
hills of Wicklow.

Lacy soon learns of Riordan's return and sets out to confront him.
On that day Riordan has left his bride to view an approaching storm
from atop a crag. Here the rivals meet, again by coincidence, and once
more Lacy survives after being hurled down the mountainside. Awakening the following evening, he is confronted by the "ghost" of his
once-betrothed who warns him to mend his ways. He swears to do so

and begs her to inform him of matters beyond the grave. Esther has her opportunity: passion and vanity, she instructs, must be abandoned before he is ever to know eternal peace. Lacy swears to change his ways and with that Esther leaves him. Later, when he regains his strength, he tries once again to best his enemy only to fail and to repent for a second time before a "resurrected" Esther.

The theme of resurrection, Riordan's return from exile, Esther's role as a ghost, Lacy's durability in combat and his inclination toward repentance, are contrasted by the realism of the opening dispensary scene in which Doctor Jarvis struggles to handle a throng of ailing peasants and one of the closing scenes of the tale in which Davy Lenigan, before his cronies at the local inn, eloquently and judiciously lodges his complaint against the British government and prescribes the Irish Catholic's best stand against it—peace and endurance. However effective these scenes are in terms of social verisimilitude and thematic relevance, Griffin's serializing of the combat between Riordan and Lacy and such scenes as the lover's spell in the burial vault render the tale hopelessly melodramatic.

Undoubtedly, Griffin felt justified in such handling of the theme of "resurrection" because he knew that Abel Tracy's "rebirth" would more than compensate his reader for the improbabilities in "The Rivals." "Tracy's Ambition" achieves distinction as an example of Griffin's ability to trace realistically a life of moral ruin and regeneration in a time of national crisis.

III *"Tracy's Ambition"*

Griffin believed a true Irishman was one who had a stake in the future of Ireland. He demonstrated his belief with a superbly written, psychologically developed story of one man's greed and ambition in a time in Ireland's history when hostilities were being stirred up by the United Irishmen and the Irish parliament passed in February, 1796, an insurrection act which "made it a capital offence to administer an unlawful oath, and empowered the lord lieutenant and privy council to proclaim any distrust as disturbed: in a district so proclaimed the magistrates were given extraordinary powers. . . ."[2] The militia was made up largely of Roman Catholics and the yeomanry came from the tenants of protestant landlords.[3] In "Tracy's Ambition" Dalton is just such a magistrate and Abel Tracy, just such a member of the yeomanry in County Kerry.

IV   *"Tracy's Ambition": Summary and Analysis*

The story involves Abel Tracy's marriage to Mary Regan, his social superior, and his subsequent attempts to improve himself during a period of tremendous political unrest and violence caused by Wolf Tone's efforts to secure an Irish government representing the majority of Ireland's inhabitants. When Abel marries Mary, her brother Ulick Regan leaves the country in disgust over the match. During the progress of Tracy's climb to power some years later, a tall, lean "yellow man" is observed in the vicinity, obviously very rich and quite intent upon helping the poor. This eccentric "yellow man" continues to appear throughout the story until in the final scenes his identity becomes known and his significance as an allegorical figure, signifying the return of Tracy's Christian conscience, becomes apparent to the reader.

Tracy's ambition is to better his present lot as a landlord's agent, that is, one who works between the landlord and the peasants securing leases and rents. He has discovered through Mr. Clancy, a friend, that a wealthy landlord and magistrate by the name of Dalton will favor him with his friendship. The association now established, Dalton borrows five hundred pounds from the dowry Tracy is about to bestow upon his daughter and Rowan Clancy, the son of Tracy's old friend. As Tracy's familiarity with Dalton grows, an alienation between him and the peasants becomes apparent until at one point because of all the coercive measures being brought to bear against the peasants by the magistrates and militia, Tracy and Dalton are attacked by ruffians and Tracy is wounded. The incident serves only to make Dalton and Tracy's relationship warmer, and during one evening's festivities while in the magistrate's company, Tracy's concept of what a true Irish gentleman is swells to the following proportions: Tracy recalls:

the truth of an observation I had heard made by many men of the world, that 'an Irish gentleman is the first gentleman on earth.' The reason, (supposing it any more than a national boast) might perhaps be found in that habitual frankness and gaiety which gives them all the air, step, and port of elder brothers; and in this abject condition of their peasantry which leaves them more of the lordly feeling and consciousness of feudal authority than is found in other and happier countries. (*T*, 191)

From this initial incursion of pride Tracy is to descend to the level of begging his daughter to marry a man she does not love in order to save her father from financial ruin.

Tracy's education under Dalton continues with the magistrate's notions of eighty percent of the population of Ireland: "The poor are not thought of here! They are taxed for work and money, and then turned off to find their own amusements, if they wish for them. And this they do in good earnest; witness their jig houses, their shebeens, their benefits and balls, their drunkenness, their factious spirit, their nightwalking, and all the turbulent and improvident vices of their character" (*T*, 197). The test of what Dalton says follows upon the slaughter of one of Tracy's tenants. Tracy, no longer close to his peasant tenants and not quite an officer of the law himself, is shaken by the threat from the mother of the victim and in the guilt he bears for the violence that is supposedly preserving law and order: "Ah, Abel Tracy," exclaims the old woman, "there is no law for the poor in Ireland, but what they make themselves" (*T*, 201). Henceforth, Tracy has to find his own way to peace of mind, and it is to be one leading to a far deeper understanding of what being an Irishman means than he has previously had under the influence of Dalton. Quartering Dalton's "Peelers" in his home and seeing the horror of his brutality in checking peasant militancy, witnessing the death of his own wife at the hands of peasant marauders, and living in constant regret for ever having thought about economic and political advancement, Tracy gropes for meaning in his present state until Clancy, who originally told Tracy about Dalton's interest in him, comes forward once again, but this time with different news: Dalton has no intention of elevating Tracy and will probably himself assume the post that he has promised to his gullible agent.

In a fury Tracy seeks Dalton and finally locates him in the city of Limerick. Here Tracy encounters a young woman whom Dalton victimized. She directs Tracy to the inn at which the magistrate is staying, and there in the dark of the room he awaits the man who has brought him so much ruin: "Here, while I stood awaiting in silence and in the agony of a deep suspense the arrival of my destroyer, and the departure of all whose presence might interfere with my design, a scene of atrocity was laid open to my view, in comparison with which all that I either had learned or suspected of Dalton's magisterial profligacy was venial, and worthy rather of pity than reproof" (*T*, 271). In this dark corner Tracy reviews his past actions and reflects upon what he intends for Dalton—killing him. But Griffin avoids melodrama in the confrontation as Tracy acts consistently through the passion he has been nurturing since first he decided upon wealth and power.

When Dalton at last returns with one of his spies, Tracy is determined to learn as much about him as possible. He listens to that interview and the one that follows between the magistrate and his informers. Once the disclosures pertaining to caches of arms and the names of those taking "croppie oaths" are made, Dalton is left to his final interview with Tracy.

Several factors account for Tracy's failure to murder Dalton: he is quite exhausted from his trip and his vigil; his charity to the young lady who had been abused by Dalton has been spiritually refreshing; and the hidden reason for the magistrate's desperate need for money is now made known to him—Dalton has been supporting his son's extravagances and the affair has cost him dearly. Consequently, Tracy loses the will to revenge himself upon Dalton, a man who is basically in Tracy's own position, and sinks completely exhausted to the floor of the inn.

The confessional tone of the entire scene is one that would immediately impress Griffin's countrymen. The ingredients of a "good confession" are here: solitude, darkness, reflection on a grievous matter, the infusion of grace and Tracy's remorse. The final stages of his regeneration are about to begin.

When Tracy is revived by the inkeeper and told that the "yellow man" has been seeking him, he locates the stranger and begs to be of service. Tracy's state of mind is suggested in his compliance to the strange man's request that Ellen, Tracy's daughter, be married immediately. Paul Purtill, the local dandy, is chosen by the anxious parent and a date is set. However, Ellen will have no part of the arrangement. Groveling before her, Tracy places his future in her hands: the man who married Mary Regan now relies on her daughter to save him from a catastrophe he cannot bear to face—financial ruin.

Melodrama closes the tale as Mary's brother, Ulick Regan, the "yellow man," steps forward and directs Ellen to marry her original choice—Rowan Clancy. Having returned from South America where he acquired his yellow pigmentation in long military service, Regan now sees confirmed his original estimation of Tracy's character. However, he in turn receives reproof for his own lack of charity in a letter Mary has left all these years to be opened by him in the event of his return. In it she confesses her love for Abel and begs her brother to accept him one day. Ulick now feels the years of wasted separation from his family and readily admits that "Mary's fault was venial; it was the fault of a moment, an error of the judgment rather than the heart" (*T*, 363). He is restored, but in his comment about Mary's "error of judgment," Tracy is seared with the realization that his great fault, ambition, was apparent to Regan from the moment of their first meet-

ing and in all its destructive potential. However, the brother who failed
to aid his sister has lived to atone for this lapse with his charitable acts
throughout the neighborhood and his reconciliation with his family.
Tracy can do no less with his remaining years.

Abel Tracy's story was begun some time before Griffin began work
on *The Collegians* and completed late in 1829 when success and fame
were proving to be meaningless to a man who, now more than ever,
was craving service to God. Yet, Tracy's character is among the first
creations of Griffin to undergo detailed psychological change, for the
most part recorded by the character himself, as he experiences two
opposing worlds—the world of the Protestant landlord and magistrate,
basing his idea of Ireland's worth on what service can be got from a
"shiftless" peasantry, and the world of the peasants, who look on
Tracy's desertion as symptomatic of the continuing failure of the Protestant ruling class to understand their position—natives of the soil they
may not possess, victims of a tyranny they may not oppose. With
"Tracy's Ambition" Griffin is beginning to evoke, in addition to a
highly moral tone, psychological realism and strong social commentary
in his presentation of the turmoil leading up to the Rebellion of 1798.
And if the presence of the "yellow man," noted at various stages of
Tracy's decline, can be accepted as a literary device, representing
Tracy's lust for gold and power, on the one hand, and his former charity, on the other, then Griffin was indeed showing fine artistic promise,
using the essential ingredient of his art—passion in the hearts of the
people he knew best.

V   The Christian Physiologist

The complete title of Griffin's tales for children is *The Christian
Physiologist. Tales Illustrative of The Five Senses: Their Mechanism,
Uses, and Government; With Moral and Explanatory Introductions.
Addressed to a Young Friend. Edited by the Author of "The Collegians," &c.*[4] In the book the speaker describes himself as a "votary of
the Gospel" and addresses a child called Cyriac in a manner befitting
an evangelist with a penchant for discovering the best approach to the
old problem of spirit versus flesh. In his prefatory remarks the speaker
sets his tone of religious revitalization: "It is absolutely certain that
there is little even of the true understanding of their eternal destinies
among men, and that few practice, or even remember in age, the principles and practice of their youth. The world, passion, and sensual
interests draw them away, and religion is almost only cherished by

children, yet faintly tempted, or by age, no longer susceptible of temptation."[5] This is the state of Ireland's spiritual household, Griffin believes, and, as the speaker, he exhorts science with all its profound erudition to humble itself and support the efforts of the church in teaching faith and morals.

Cyriac, whose sole identity rests in the fact that he is a lad in search of a good catechism, receives the speaker's own learned essays on the five senses, hopefully to suffice until more adequate material becomes available. The total "scientific" content of *The Christian Physiologist* is supposed to impress young readers with, basically, the fact that the senses are material faculties and that, therefore, their operation is affected or conditioned by many factors. In the fiction following each essay on a particular sense, these factors are dealt with in terms of the operation of the intellect as it deals with subjective and objective realities. For example, "The Kelp Gatherer" treats the sense of sight as Griffin, the "physiologist," attempts to demonstrate the relativity of sensation, that is, how seeing is related to various physical laws which condition the manner in which objects are perceived. He impresses the reader with the fact that man is composed of mind and body whose interaction has the most profound influence on sense perception. His tales present very clear and precise actions designed to show that man's power to know is based on sensory perception and the principles of moral actions that he brings to bear upon sense data. Hence, there is vivid imagery and striking religious tone in each tale's introduction. That of "The Kelp Gatherer," selected to represent the author's acute didactic purpose in this collection, offers the best example.

VI   *"The Kelp Gatherer"*

"The Kelp Gatherer" opens with a grim reminder of the precarious life of the Irish peasant, and of the harsh world in which he must sustain himself.

The Stranger who wanders along the terrific masses of crag that overhang the green and foaming waters of the Atlantic on the western coasts of Ireland, feels a melancholy interest excited in his mind, as he turns aside from the more impressive grandeurs of the scene, and gazes on the small stone heaps that are scattered over the moss on which he treads. They are the graves of the nameless few whose bodies have been from time to time rejected from the bosom of the ocean, and cast upon these lonely crags to startle the early fishermen with their ghastly and disfigured bulk.[6]

Somber imagery of hard life and imminent death begins this tale of a mother and her only son barely sustaining life by their occupation of gathering kelp for the manufacture of soap along the precipitous Atlantic coast of County Clare.

VII *"The Kelp Gatherer": Summary and Analysis*

When Richard Reardon attains manhood, he resolves to set off for America to make his fortune and to return to relieve the burden of his mother's last years. In her son's absence, Mrs. Reardon never allows her devotion to God to pale in her deep affection for her son until she learns that he is about to return. In that moment she forgets her reliance upon divine will and allows the seemingly unceasing storms that suddenly arise to inform her of impending doom. In her sleep she continues to imagine the worst will happen. Opinion from neighbors directs her to believe that homeward bound ships seldom meet fair weather. When her son and his American family finally arrive at the old woman's door, they find her blind. The calamity, however, has restored Mrs. Reardon's attention to God, first in all things, as she confesses to her son that she has thought too much of him and is now chastened. Happy in her Maker's will, she argues that she can still "see" Richard and that he too must be content. News of her affliction reaches a local surgeon who examines Mrs. Reardon and proposes an operation to check the disease of cataract. After the operation's successful conclusion when the mother views her son once more, details of his and his family's appearance are disclosed for the first time suggesting the delight felt at the return of a lost blessing. In the mother's words to her son concerning her judging "aright," Griffin distinguishes logical truth from moral truth: the doctor's diagnosis is logical; the neighbors' opinions are immoral, since what they say has no substance in fact and is certainly alien to the physical laws of nature. Mrs. Reardon's judgment about God's will is based on a principle: she learns what she should do about her blindness, namely, accept God's will and His providence, and she acts after her judgment is made. Griffin also demonstrates physical certitude and moral certitude in the action of the doctor and the faithful kelp gatherer. He distinguishes between opinion which is based on partial evidence and certitude which excludes fear of error.

In "The Kelp Gatherer," Griffin stresses the complexity of man's physical and moral existence, moving his tender readers to a conclusion that spirit and matter can be joined in harmony when individuals continue to be aware of how they acquire knowledge and make judgments. The will causes error in human judgment when it forces the individual to "create" evidence which does not exist. Motivation of the will to act in this manner emanates from such personal factors as passions and prejudices. Such is the moral content and tedium in this, the best of the tales.

Of the others, dealing with the remaining four senses, three are little more than outcroppings from his research into Irish medieval history in preparation for *The Invasion*, while one remains an allegory on the needs of a Christian intellect. "The Voluptuary Cured" treats a more familiar scene in which a young absentee landlord returns to his homeland after years of dissipation abroad to find his body's and his soul's cure in the restoration of his destitute and long-suffering people. "The Day of the Trial," set in the Meath of medieval times, is the story of God's gift of speech and hearing to a boy who prayed for his father's welfare. A luxury-minded prince of Meath, in "The Self-Consumed," is checked by the story of a maniac who once, as court poet, fell in love with his queen and suffered banishment. "The Selfish Crotarie," concerns a harper whose bibulous ways account for the destruction of a monastery by the Vikings and for his own death. With "A Story of Psyche," Griffin provides his young readers with an allegory of how Psyche—the intellectual—discovered that "Imagination" and the virgins, "Faith," "Hope," and "Charity," could restore her to God's graces.

In the year *The Christian Physiologist* was published (1830), Griffin wrote from seclusion in Pallas Kenry that his passion for writing was all but dead, but that the preceding year, the year he first met Lydia Fisher, "made me think I had the elements of contentment about me."[7] The intensely religious tone of *The Christian Physiologist* and the preparatory course he was pursuing for admission to the College of Maynooth seem clear indications that his "contentment" of 1829 had precipitated changes in the life and work of this scrupulous young man.

VIII   The Invasion

Gerald's experiment with purely religious matter proved to be a failure, but his dedication to the "perfectly moral" novel continued. The publication of *The Invasion* two years later, 1832, carried with it the air of accomplishment. It was not completed in haste as most of his previous writing. His research had been thorough; his purpose noble— to acquaint his people with "some of the influences which have con-

curred in the formation of the national character";[8] his attitude pomp-
ous. This "moral history" neither ennobled his countrymen nor justified his posture as moral arbiter. A single part of this would-be epic
possesses "life," occasionally, in Kenric, the frustrated scholar and
lover.

Griffin believed that the story's scope encompassing eighth-century
Ireland (Inisfail, in the text), England (Inismore), and Sweden (Sitheod)
with accompanying exotic scenes of Druid and Norse temples and
combat among Vikings, Celts, and Druids would entice some readers,
while the parallel story lines, of Elim, the Celtic chieftain, and Kenric,
the Anglo-Saxon scholar, might appeal to others. But his political ser-
monizing echoed similar conservative voices on both sides of the Irish
Sea while the analogies he drew between eighth-century Ireland and
England and present times competed with the fever and excitement
O'Connell was generating in the field. The story itself posed a difficult
problem for his readers: for all of its exoticism, pageantry and action,
it is defeated by insipid, two-dimensional characters in mask and costume. Ironically, his characters suggest the artificiality he himself
deplored when first he viewed the London stage in 1823. A further
obstacle arises from the fact that the book abounds with the notes he
gathered so assiduously at the London and Dublin libraries on ninth-
century Gaelic and Nordic social and political institutions. He wanted
his readers to appreciate the fact that the Irish were once a proud and
noble race, who, for example, sent scholars to the far corners of Chris-
tendom during the Middle Ages. What he hoped for most in Elim, the
Celtic chieftain, and Kenric, the Northumbrian scholar, was that *The
Invasion* would provide all Irishmen with a knowledge of their country's glorious past and a lesson from her history of disunity.

IX   The Invasion: *Summary and Analysis*

The time of the story is approximately the beginning of the ninth
century when Charlemagne became Holy Roman Emperor. The
locales range from southwestern Ireland to England and the eastern
coast of Sweden. The opening scene is filled with pageantry as two
Celtic septs (or clans) celebrate their alliance in the marriage of the
chieftain O'Haedha to Macha, a neighboring chieftain's daughter.
While these festivities are taking place, Griffin fails to comment on the
Druid threat so close at hand. A continuing menace because they have
not been given equality under Celtic law, the Druids, according to the
story, resist conversion to the Catholic faith and carry on sporadic war-

fare with their conquerors. In one such battle, O'Haedha is killed and
Macha, his wife, vows that Elim, their son, will be a "wiser" chieftain.
Therefore, she sends the boy to the famous abbey at Muingharid (Mun-
gret, near Limerick on the Shannon shore) and there Elim meets Kenric, the strange, close-cropped Northumbrian sent from England to
Muingharid for an education he apparently failed to receive at the
hands of his uncle, Vuscfraea, a stern teacher of Latin. The theme of
education begins as Griffin contrasts the two boys, their backgrounds,
and their progress at the abbey school.

Elim is wise, strong, athletic, and humble in his success while Kenric
remains superior in scholarship alone, so much so that learning
becomes a passion distorting his image of even Elim, his best friend.
Griffin makes his point about education for the young in his description
of the activities at the famous abbey school: in this school of two thousand young men the philosophy of education calls for students to study,
to work, and to play according to Christian principles of love and obedience to authority. The discipline promotes Elim's finest qualities, but
Kenric's ruinous career of vanity and pride soon erupts. The two
friends separate, Elim to his home to assume his duties as chieftain and
Kenric to find employment as a teacher. At this point Griffin traces
separately the lives of these two men who eventually meet again, in
time of national crisis for Ireland, to renew their friendship, Kenric
with a much chastened heart.

Elim's home and his fortress are located in the area of Bantry Bay
in southwest Ireland (surrounded by beautifully rugged mountains
once explored by Griffin in the company of James and Lydia Fisher).
Once home, Elim assumes power after he expels Baseg, one of his
father's old comrades who in his contest with Elim represents the
unenlightened order that creates factions within the clan and perpetuates strife with the neighboring Druids. Many years later Baseg is to
lead a Viking expedition to Bantry Bay and to have his final trial with
Elim.

As Elim works to promote the welfare of his people, Kenric's pride
destroys his chances to work for Alcuin, Charlemagne's scholar. The
haughty young man hears no voice but his own and soon finds himself
on the road and in the company of Inguar, a Swede, who in telling his
life's story makes the people, villages, temples, and warriors of Upsal
(Uppsala) strikingly resemble the status quo in southwest Ireland. Griffin's intention is to show that Christians resemble pagans when they
worship the same gods of slaughter.

Inguar leaves Kenric to join the Vikings who are planning to raid the English coast. Kenric secures a teaching post in East Anglia where he meets Baseg and falls under the influence of the old man's story of being deprived of his rights to rule in his country. Kenric at this time does not realize Baseg's enemy is Elim, and so before leaving Baseg and his preparation for an invasion, he takes an oath to support the old man in his ambition.

As Kenric and Inguar first make their acquaintance, Elim discovers Eithne, the beautiful Christian daughter of the Druid chieftain's brother. Elim has been captured by the Druids on one of their raids and Eithne uses her influence to set him free once she discovers that his foresight and wisdom could bring peace to their troubled land. The two soon fall in love, apparently on the basis that their political philosophies are so ideally mated, and Elim is off to England to secure the blessing of the old patron of Eithne's father living there in exile. Fortunately for Kenric, Elim meets his old school friend, who has lost his teaching position, in time to save him from death through starvation and exposure. Kenric has been too proud to return to his parents, a father who has scorned his learning and a mother who has doted on him. Elim manages to check his friend's pride momentarily and the family is reunited before the two collegians set off for Ireland and the parliament at Tara, which is being held to decide the best measures for defense against a probable Viking invasion.

At the parliament Kenric sees his friend's greatness as a leader and statesman. Elim speaks for unity and accord to meet the threats from within Ireland and from the invaders. At this conclave Kenric also meets Eithne and begins to court her, not knowing that she is Elim's betrothed. Quite upset when the disclosure is finally made, Kenric departs, only to be met by Inguar in Baseg's service. The old Celt has enlisted not only Vikings and Anglo-Saxons but Druids as well. A further design in his revenge upon Elim is his wish that Kenric marry Eithne, who is now his prisoner. Kenric renounces his oath to the old man at this juncture and flees to warn Elim, who finally arrives to crush the invasion and kill Baseg. When order and harmony are restored, Kenric bids farewell to his friends for the last time, returning to his home in England where he soon, in a semidelirious state, confesses his spirit of pride to be broken and his miserable and ungrateful life nearly ended. It is interesting to note that Elim and Eithne's marriage is the single factor responsible for crushing Kenric's pride. From an autobiographical point of view, Griffin felt very much like Kenric in that he too would always be, to Lydia, "less than a lover."

The Invasion was Griffin's greatest effort. He was too serious an art-

ist here to allow all his effort to become what John Cronin describes as
a "kind of patriotic escapism, a flight from the harsh realities of an
intolerable Irish present to the halcyon days of a glorious past."[9]
Although he confessed that writing the book would be of personal service to himself, the preponderance of contemporary political overtones, in addition to the outlay of his other public and private themes,
placed the book very much with the times in which he was writing.
Griffin, here, was a pious propagandist intent on defining Irish pride
and promoting peace.

His style is grandiose: politics, nationalism, and antiquarianism fill
a story of epic proportions but one which fails to sustain such bulk
because of weak characterizations; moreover, the peasants who live
close to the fortresses and temples are seldom seen. Instead of characters, Griffin provides names for his several voices—political, moral, historical, personal. *The Invasion* in the "objective correlative" for Griffin's feelings about invasions which take place not only on the shores
of countries throughout the world but in the hearts and minds of individuals: the invasion of pride, for example, which in crippling private
conscience endangers society as a whole. This kind of theme in no way
suggests "patriotic escapism."

To a large extent, the book is about Kenric, another solitary figure
like Cregan, Tracy, Hamond, and Dinny Macnamara. Kenric's pride
is founded on the fame that his treatise upon the stars brings to him.
However, after learning the futility of such pride through his experiences with Elim, whose eyes are upon his people and their problems,
Kenric comes to speak as Griffin would have all Irishmen speak. In
spurning Inguar's offer to join Baseg's forces against Elim, the Anglo-
Saxon exclaims: "Renounce my friend, my country (for it is in part my
country), aye—and her faith, to pleasure thee and Baseg" (*I*, 348). One
reason for Kenric's conversion is the fact that the Anglo-Saxon knows
how inextricably the destinies of the two islands are bound. In one of
his first encounters with the students of the abbey school at
Muingharid, Kenric displays his awareness of Anglo-Irish economics,
still very much the case today. A student assails Kenric:

"Anglo-Saxon, if the Praelector sees thee with that short crop, he will not
leave thee long in the enjoyment of it. He'll make an Irishman of thee, in that
respect."

Kenric, who had by this time recovered his natural spirits, replied with
readiness:

"Neither head nor foot, shall thy Praelector ever make an Irishman of me.
An Anglo-Saxon I was born, and an Anglo-Saxon I will die."

"Aye," said the other, looking back, "if thy father do not sell thee to some ceannuighe [merchant] of Port Lairge [Waterford] for a load of peltry and an Irish hound."

Kenric blushed deeply at this allusion to a disgraceful species of traffic at that time carried on between the islands.

"Thou mightest have spared," he said, "a reproach that but half reaches me. If there be sellers in England, there are buyers in Inisfail, so the shame is even betwixt us." (*I*, 47)

Kenric knows this much about political economy, and Elim knows how best to serve his own people by answering their immediate material needs, by adjusting the laws of property and succession so that a man can call his land his own. In one discussion with Kenric after Elim has assumed control of his sept, Elim tells his friend what he has discovered about the nature of those whom he rules:

Men are so jealous of authority, even of their own creation; there is such a spirit of selfish pride in our nature, such a difficulty in adknowledging a superior, that it is dangerous to force us, even to our own advantage. Many a more potent governor than O'Haedha has lost his people's confidence, and his own power, to an impatience for their welfare, and a want of care in considering their prejudices. It is also certain, perhaps owing to the same jealousy, that the capability of doing public good, diminishes in proportion as the extent of the sovereign's authority increases. (*I*, 136)

Elim concludes his speech by telling Kenric "that a governor who wishes to promote the real advantage of his people, must often sacrifice his views to theirs, when they do not violate principles that are immutable" (*I*, 137). Eithne, Elim's future bride, knows from her vantage point within a Druid stronghold the truth of Elim's statement. She confesses:

Though I mourn, deeply mourn, the fallen honour of my race, I could well behold them still more straightened in power, provided their depression could contribute in any degree to promote union and good-will amongst the bickering children of our common country. I know, woman though I am, I know how this will end. The hand of the Dal Cais will be raised against the Eoganacht, Uladh will make war on Midhe, and Claire on Connacht, the spirit of dissension will divide our princes, from the Ard-righ of Erinn to the poorest chieftain of a distant township; some foreign foe will take advantage of their discord, and Erinn never—never more will know what freedom is. (*I*, 93)

This is Griffin's political voice, one sponsored to a great extent by the work of the Catholic Association and its leader Daniel O'Connell.

Griffin made his book into a treatise on solving the ills of contemporary Ireland. "Union and love," words sung by Eithne to Elim and before a Druid audience, are rather empty without some understanding of Ireland's glorious past, the author felt. Druid and Celt, in this fiction, learn to live in peace and harmony, and part of their ability to do so is through an understanding of each other's values and heritages. Griffin's attempts at placing his readers in ninth-century Ireland involve scenes depicting marriage, burial, battle, and government, but they succeed only in impeding the story's progress and deadening characterizations. One character escapes the effects of this antiquarianism and lifeless characterization. Kenric vacillates between pride and humility as his love for Eithne and his friendship for Elim seek accord. When Kenric falls hopelessly in love with Eithne, his pride in learning is unable to sustain him. In bestowing his treatise upon the stars to Eithne as a memento at their parting, Kenric despairs in further living. The delirium in which he dies—calling for all the great scholars of the world to bear him to his grave with the stipulation that he be buried at the feet of his mother—is convincing in view of Griffin's careful attention to Kenric and his parents' relationship throughout the text. Both parents of the scholar change as a result of their son's pride and his flagrant abuse of them. Ailred, his father, turns from an irascible, ineffectual tyrant to a submissive and pathetic sight at the side of his dying son. Domnona, his mother, realizes through the pain Kenric has inflicted upon her, how she has failed in raising her son.

The autobiographical aspect of Kenric's image is apparent once he makes contact with Eithne at the great Feis or parliament of chieftains. At that meeting, Kenric seems to suggest Griffin when the latter first met Lydia Fisher and his wanderings seemed to come to an end. Leon Edel's observations on the literary artist and on the autobiographical aspect of his work are relevant to a fuller understanding of Griffin's motivations.

Psychoanalysis assumes that creative writers do their work out of profound inner dictates and in response to the ways in which their emotions and their views of the world have been formed. With all the world to choose from, they invariably select subjects closest to their inner feelings; and when they choose subjects seemingly alien to them, they invariably alter them to correspond to their personal condition, even though what emerges may seem, to the uninitiated, remote and unrelated. This is a fundamental belief of the modern study of behavior; and we can state it as a literary axiom. The subject selected by an artist more often than not reveals some emotion the writer had to express, some state of feeling, some view of life, some inner conflict or state of disequilibrium in his being, which sought resolution in the form of art. In this sense it might be said that writers—and writers of fiction in particular—are always engaged in creating parables about themselves.[10]

The triangle of Elim, Eithne, and Kenric appears to be an example of Professor Edel's point about a literary artist expressing some aspect of his "personal condition" in his writing. Griffin's being "less than a lover, and more than a friend" to Lydia Fisher seems to be reflected in the despair and death of Kenric. Griffin creates Kenric's despair from the proud Anglo-Saxon's failure to succeed as a scholar and teacher, but he signals Kenric's end precisely at the moment of Elim and Eithne's marriage. No other event in the novel affects Kenric as does the marriage of Eithne and Elim. And the position in which Griffin found himself in 1829—in love with another man's wife—was as fulfilling emotionally and intellectually as it was excruciatingly painful. In view of this situation with the Fishers, his devoted friends, he continued to write out his decision to quit art with one artistic failure after another. The operation took nearly eight years and in that time there were moments when his genius resisted the imposed sentence to die to art.

The works discussed in this chapter attest to the moral petrifaction that his conservatism in his writing was dictating. He had abandoned the successful formula he discovered in writing *The Collegians* because of the strain it placed on his spiritual well-being. The tension in his life concerning matters spiritual and temporal is that which creates Abel Tracy and suggests the penitential value that writing *The Christian Physiologist* must have had upon his overbearing scrupulosity. Elim's and Kenric's love of the same woman is Griffin's last artistic expression, conscious or otherwise, of his love for Lydia Fisher. These works, then, seem to close that period of his writing career wherein can be glimpsed the most remarkable signs of his struggle with art and religion.

CHAPTER 7

The Neighborhood

FROM 1830 to 1838, between his family home in Pallas Kenry and his bachelor quarters in Limerick, Gerald did little other than write about his neighborhood and travel principally to England and Scotland. In 1832 he was thrilled to meet the poet Thomas Moore at his English home. The electors of Limerick had asked Gerald, who was going to London on business, to stop at Sloperton Cottage and ask the poet to stand for representative of the city. Moore declined the invitation but extended one of his own to the young novelist. Six years later, Gerald toured Scotland in the company of his brother Daniel.

During this period of eight years, As Griffin enjoyed the security of his family and the familiarity of local scenes, he wrote his last works: *Tales of My Neighbourhood* (1835), *The Duke of Monmouth* (1836), and, published posthumously, *Talis Qualis; or, Tales of the Jury Room* (1842). For the most part, the tone of *Tales of My Neighbourhood* is one of social satire, a vein never before approached with such a light heart and in such breadth. His Limerick neighbors posed and he recorded them in light, humorous, didactic strokes. All classes and types came under the close scrutiny of an artist who was obviously enjoying what he was writing.

I Tales of My Neighbourhood

"The Barber of Bantry," the first of thirteen tales in this collection and by far the longest and most entertaining, consists of two loosely joined stories—the first concerning the lives of three generations of Moynihans and the second treating that of O'Berne, the barber. From the chaotic and yet interrelated rush of anecdotes delivered by characters in the first half of "The Barber of Bantry" to the remaining twelve tales in which character cross-references and reappearances reinforce the theme of social and moral instability, Griffin produces for his reader a growing familiarity with the character of a neighborhood through ever-widening disclosures about its inhabitants.

Tales of My Neighbourhood spans one century of "our neighbours'" lives from the beginning of Penal days in 1700 to the present time of Griffin's writing. His peasants, middlemen, and Protestant gentry possess the same strengths and weaknesses throughout. Problems and solutions remain the same. All that seems to matter to the author is that there is time for retribution, reconciliation, and charity in the lives of his characters once they learn the error of their ways. Social unity emerges as the central theme from folklore, realism, caricatures, and melodrama, suggesting Griffin's awareness that if he were to influence his people in matters of social reform as they were striking for religious and political freedom, then his material had to be close to home, immediately recognizable. *The Invasion's* failure was his proof.

II *"The Barber of Bantry": Summary and Analysis*

The *Tales* focus on Griffin's best "character," his Limerick neighborhood for which he was attempting to establish a conscience, and "The Barber of Bantry" represents his best efforts in this direction.

"The Barber" involves three generations of Moynihans who are ruined through their ignorance, superstition, extravagance, and dissipation, and O'Berne, the barber, whose somnambulistic adventures resolve the mystery of the disappearance of the last of the Moynihans. The story of Patrick Moynihan, the first master of "Tipsy Hall," is told by Griffin and characters in the tale. Moynihan's ignominious end, participated in by the same people who once crowded his table to toast his health and prosperity, comes at the auction of his house furnishings. Rich Lillis, Patrick's servant, narrates the story of the master's son, Henry Moynihan. Here the volume of dialogue increases as the character of the breed is placed in somewhat clearer focus by Rich's single anecdote: Griffin has moved his readers from the blurred reports of gossips at Patrick's table to a single encounter in the life of Henry.

A favorite mare of the master has died and, upon the advice of Rick, Shaun Dooly, "a knowledgeable man that lived down near the say-side, that had a great report for bein thick with the good people"[1] is brought to Henry Moynihan for advice:

I brought Shaun Dooly up to the masther, and he seemed for a while greatly puzzled to know what could be the cause of it. "Did you ever shoat a weasel?" says Shaun Dooly. "Not to my knowledge," says the masther. "Or a magpie?" "Not as I remember, indeed." "Do you be whistlin' when you do be out at night at all?" "That can't be," says the masther, "For I never turned a tune,"

"Well I don't know in the world what to think of it" says Shaun. So while he was thinkin' there was a great flutterin' outside. "What's that noise?" says Shaun Dooly. "I suppose it's the pigeons that's comin' home," says the masther. "Pigeons!" cries Shaun, "do you keep pigeons about the house? It's plain to me now," says he, "what rason your mare died, an' I would'nt wondher," says he, "if all belongin' to you was gone to rack and ruin." "What rason?" says the masther. "I'll not tell you what rason," says Shaun, "but if you take my advice, you'll not have one of 'em about the place." He went, an' next mornin' early the masther went about shootin' all the pigeons. There was one of 'em that Dumby had tamed, an' when he seen 'em all shootin', he took an' hid it from the masther, poor crathur, it was so quiet an' so fond of him. Well, sure enough in less than two months afther the ould missiz died an' the masther found out that the Dumby kept the pigeon. I never seen one so wild. He turned the Dumby out o' doors (although the crathur cried a gallonfull, an' went on his knees to ax pardon), an' twisted the head off o' the pigeon. But it was no good for him. From that day out it seemed as if the loock went out o' the doores with the Dumby. And when the next Mr. Moynihan came into the property, he found himself much in the situation of more jentlemen in the country then an' now, that have 'pon my honour, an' nothing to back it. (N, 71–74)

The expulsion of a peasant from a master's household means extreme hardship, even death from exposure or starvation, in these early Penal days. The moral and the humor in Rich's anecdote are reminders that there are few substitutes for charity and understanding, particularly in times of social crisis.

The fall of Edmond Moynihan, the last of the masters of "Tipsy Hall," is traced by the original narrator. Edmond and his wife live exemplary lives until the Tobins move into the neighborhood and Edmond becomes a frequent visitor and finally one of Tobin's drunken cronies. Contributing to Edmond's instability at this time is his sudden elevation to the position of tax-gatherer, which puts him in touch with the economics of a hidden Gaelic world he never dreamed existed. However, before his carousing with Tobin begins or cynicism at his neighbors' undeclared wealth infects him, Edmond and his wife are able to put "Tipsy Hall" in order. The time now is close to the end of the eighteenth century, just prior to the Act of Union (1800), which brought Ireland under direct control of the British Parliament.

The tale of O'Berne, the barber of Bantry, is coupled to the mysterious disappearance of the tax-gatherer on the stormy night he leaves Tobin's home in possession of five hundred pounds and a liberal quantity of whiskey punch and stops at O'Berne's shop on his way home.

However, before this incident occurs, the narrator provides O'Berne's background. As a boy he was delivered by his father into the hands of a rich, eccentric old man to receive an education. During the six years O'Berne remained with his benefactor, he was encouraged to read philosophical works exclusively. From the experience O'Berne emerged reserved, sheepish, and abrupt. Such behavior soon drew ridicule from local wags and, from the community at large, a small clientele as he followed his father's occupation of barber. One other fact about O'Berne's character becomes apparent: he is readily impressed by what he hears, letting others' thoughts overshadow and tinge his own. Fortunately, however, O'Berne marries Mary Renahan whose cheer and beauty soon cause the barber to become more practical and industrious. While still drawing abuse from the village bullies, the barber's happiness with his wife and children continues to grow until he and then Mary and the children are struck by a typhus epidemic. Added to this misery is the fact that his business nearly collapses when another barber opens his shop in the neighborhood. Through all this adversity Mary never loses her courage or cheer, so secure is she in her belief in divine providence. O'Berne's philosophical studies never prepared him for such a test, and Mary strives to convert his melancholy speculations to her own religious beliefs. The narrator comments on the philosophic barber: "His imagination became deeply impressed, and he brooded by day and dreamed by night on what he had been studying, until the whole mind became absorbed with one engrossing subject. To change the heart, it is not sufficient that the mind should be excited. To create a spirit of tenderness and love is of far greater importance in the way of virtue, than to captivate the fancy or amaze the understanding" (*N*, 196). Griffin dramatizes the meaning of what his narrator is saying by the events which immediately precede and follow the visitation of Edmond Moynihan to O'Berne's shop. One night O'Berne dreams he is visited by a stranger who resembles his old master. On the following night Edmond Moynihan pays his call.

The tax-gatherer, fresh from his debauch at Castle Tobin, rouses the barber and his wife from their sleep and in his stupor blurts out, ironically for himself, his confession about his own encounters with "phantoms": "I confess to you, there is not a single four-wheeled carriage, nor a gig, nor a riding horse in the whole neighborhood of B———. Those are all phantoms that we meet every day upon the roads—phantoms—Madam—phantoms—I have the best authority for it—the word of the owners themselves—all ghosts of greyhounds—ghosts of poverty, ghosts of spaniels, terriers, servants and all. Oh, Mrs. O'Berne, there's nothing on this island but ghosts and rogues!" (*N*, 210–11). In dealing with the subject of undeclared taxable wealth and Edmond Moynihan's part in the felonious deception, Griffin asks the moral question: do two wrongs make a right? Irishmen are living luxuriously in full view of one another but in the eyes of the king's servant their wealth remains "hidden," for the principal means by which their lives are made merry, reckless, improvident, and lawless is through smuggling. Equally "hidden" for over one hundred years is justice for Irishmen who might have escaped being "ghosts" and "rogues."

After Moynihan passes out in the barber's chair and Mary retires to bed, O'Berne takes the tax-gatherer's money and puts it aside for safekeeping fearing that Moynihan is in no condition to prevent his being robbed. He then wakes the worthy official and sends him on his way. Shortly after he retires he begins to sleepwalk in the meadow behind the shop and is brought to his senses as two of Tobin's followers strike down Moynihan and flee after finding no money. O'Berne immediately buries the body and in the morning tells his wife that Moynihan has loaned him funds to relocate and start afresh. Twenty years later O'Berne returns to make restitution. By coincindence, young Edward Moynihan, the tax-gatherer's son, happens upon the old barber and offers him temporary lodging. Without disclosing his identity O'Berne draws Edward into a discussion of restitution, and so deeply affected is the old man's conscience that in the morning he is discovered by young Moynihan sleepwalking outside the cottage. Upon questioning the old man, Edward learns the truth of his father's disappearance, convinces O'Berne that all will be well, and hastens to bury his father's bones in consecrated ground. O'Berne's peace has come at last, following his contrition and restitution. Edward Moynihan has the "loock" that his grandfather lost because he has managed his life according to Christian principles of living. Griffin's narrators, originating in the rush of gossips' reports at "Tipsy Hall" and proceeding to the final authoritative one at story's end, appear to be the outstanding feature of this diptych. His design is in the ordering of voices: when we free ourselves from such encumbrances as superstitition, false learning, gossip, and ignorance to hear the clear voice of conscience, our return to peace of mind is assured.

Griffin's writing was now a part of a greater effort—to direct his life anew. He spent three years writing and collecting *Tales of My Neighbourhood,* and in this time correspondence with Mrs. Fisher continued, but judging from the tone of the few letters written from Pallas Kenry between 1830 and 1835, Gerald had reduced his passion for Lydia's company considerably. In an undated letter in the biography immediately following one dated March 31, 1833, Gerald wrote: "And now, why does dear L—— [Lydia] talk of reluctance to send her free thoughts to her affectionate friend, and doubt of the spirit in which such affectionate and generous counsel would be taken? How could it be taken, except with gratitude, warm gratitude, to the writer, and happiness in the thought of possessing a friend so kind and so interested?"[2] His role as a writer was becoming that of a monk in the seclusion of his garden retreat, a tiny cabin behind his Pallas Kenry home in which he wrote and prayed.

With the exception of Griffin's artful manipulation of the narrators in "The Barber of Bantry" and the full, dramatic play of his peasants in the tale of an Irish feud in "The Black Birds and Yellow Hammers," *Tales of My Neighbourhood* adds little to the artistic credits of the Irish novelist. The remaining tales are exercises, some charming, others dull and even exasperating in their heavy inlay of melodrama and threadbare themes. For example, "The Great House" is a short, precisely balanced tale about a familiar figure in Ireland during the opening decades of the nineteenth century—the Catholic merchant. The commercial activities of Ireland were being handled increasingly by Catholics who began to assume the merchant's role in the preceding century when trade had been treated scornfully by the Protestant aristocracy. Peter Guerin is a member of this Catholic merchant ascendancy, and his dinner engagement at the great house, Peppercorn Hall, proves to be amusing satire as the merchant, having initially mistaken Peppercorn's retainers for members of the party, continues his efforts to peddle his wares among the distinguished guests. In "The Force of Conscience" and "The Sun-Stroke," Griffin is once again striking at courts of law in Limerick and London that he knew intimately from his days as a court reporter. Conviction through circumstantial evidence had been a curse for Irishmen for over a century, and Griffin was continuing his personal assault on magistrates and judges who refused to operate on the principle of a defendant's innocence in view of any reasonable doubt. With Mimosa M'Orient of "Mount Orient" Griffin treats once again the theme of charity as he directs Mimosa to the awareness that weeping over Ireland's ills will not feed the poor who are daily being spurned at the door of Castle M'Orient. Closing the series, "The Black Birds and Yellow Hammers" offers the social verisimilitude of earlier works with its treatment of the Irish feud. Griffin leads a throng of drinking, fighting, feuding peasants to the doors of Protestant landlords who are in the practice of educating only those of their Catholic tenants who attend Protestant services. Peasant dialogue manages story and moral from beginning to end, a felicitous feature quite rare in Griffin's fiction.

Tales of My Neighbourhood was a part of the distillation of Gerald's peace, prayer, and work at Pallas Kenry from 1830 to 1835. Settling upon his subject with a mind at rest about the future, he wrote about a landscape and a people he knew from childhood. For the most part, his tales are thematically linked. They complement and reinforce one another and, generally, in a light, satiric tone Griffin conveys his message that his neighborhood is wholesome but flawed, that it holds a very special place in his heart, that it possesses in the practice of Christian charity its own power for moral regeneration. His choice of seventeenth-century England for the scene of his next book was a matter of seeing what he could do with a popular subject of the day—the fate of James Scott, the duke of Monmouth.

III   The Duke of Monmouth

In November, 1681, John Dryden addressed the reader of "Absalom and Achitophel," a poem dealing with the ambition of the illegitimate son of Charles II, the duke of Monmouth: "The true end of Satyre, is the amendment of Vices by correction. And he who writes Honestly, is no more an Enemy to the Offendour, than the Physician to the Patient, when he prescribes harsh Remedies to an inveterate Disease. . . ."[3] Griffin was no less a "Physician" when he chose the figure of Monmouth to outline the pride and ambition in one who might bring untold misery to so many. Dryden asks the questions,

> Did ever men forsake their present ease,
> In midst of health Imagine a disease;
> Take pains Contingent mischiefs to forsee,
> Make Heirs for Monarks, and for God decree?
> What shall we think! can People give away
> Both for themselves and Sons, their Native
>   sway?

Then he answers, "Then they are left Defenseless, to the Sword/Of each unbounded Arbitrary Lord."[4] Griffin answered his people who had realized one victory, the Catholic Emancipation Act of 1829, and were in need of more prudent direction than Daniel O'Connell was offering at the time. Beckett writes:

The Roman Catholic middle classes were . . . cautious. They had fought for Emancipation as a means of gaining political power and a share of public appointments; and now they wanted to enjoy the fruits of victory, not plunge into another agitation that could only alienate the very people to whom they must look for advancement. . . . The general state of the country provided another argument in favour of delay, many reforms, social and political, were obviously and urgently necessary; and it might seem more sensible to work for these, by pressure in parliament, than to plunge the whole country into a fresh agitation.[5]

The Duke of Monmouth is a dramatization of the effects that inordinate pride and ambition in national leaders rain upon their followers. In focusing upon the similarity between the Irish in the nineteenth century and the people of southwest England who rallied to Monmouth's cause, Griffin meant to guide his readers to an understanding that Daniel O'Connell's policies of reform and repeal of union were as divisive and ruinous for the people of Ireland as was Monmouth's rebellion for the depressed and poverty-stricken people of the woollen towns of southwest England.[6]

IV   The Duke of Monmouth: *Summary and Analysis*

Griffin attempts to fuse the story of the Fullartons and Kingslys of Taunton, England, with the history of Monmouth's move from Holland in 1685 to his landing at Lyme Regis on the southwest coast of England. As Whigs, the Fullartons oppose the Kingslys, who are Royalists, until the duke, in all his folly, makes it plain on what side they all should be.

Sidney and Gaspar Fullarton, two Scotchmen, leave their native soil, Sidney to join the duke of Argyle and the duke of Monmouth in Holland, and Gaspar to settle with his family in Taunton, England. Gaspar's son Arthur and his daughter Aquila support Argyle and Monmouth passionately. In their neighborhood, Captain Kingsly is notorious for his fierce loyalty to James II while his son Henry and daughter Tamsen remain conservative and enlightened in their loyalty to the monarch. When Henry and Aquila fall in love and Arthur is attracted to Tamsen, old Kingsly rages against having any Whig in his family. At the moment Henry and Aquila are to marry, Uncle Sidney sends word for Arthur to join him in Holland. By now news of Monmouth's impending invasion is dividing the countryside, and in nine scenes dealing with the reactions of the people to political, social, economic, and religious implications of Monmouth's actions, Griffin shows his people by analogy what following O'Connor in his proposals for repeal of union might mean.

This impoverished plot closes as Aquila soon realizes her mistake in defending the traitor Monmouth against Henry's arguments based on the history of the duke's treasonable actions; Arthur loses his life to the infamous Colonel Kirke, whom he had offended when the latter made advances upon Aquila; and Aquila herself is finally driven mad when she is forced to marry Kirke to save her brother, who has already been executed. The duke's party, consisting of Fletcher, his chief advisor and a devout Republican, Lord Grey, his ineffectual general but loyal supporter, and Ferguson, an equally honest but deluded follower of the profligate, would-be monarch, fails to create either suspense or dramatic tension for the reader, who is shunted from one camp to another and exposed to bits of dialogue from a class with whom Griffin had no experience. Although Griffin followed closely the actual history of Monmouth's rebellious landing and his subsequent defeat at Sedgemoor, his protrayals of Monmouth and his cohorts are complete failures. There is, for example, never a moment when they convince the reader of the magnitude of their adventure or of their ability to carry if off.

Credibility resides at the "Three Crowns Inn," however, as Griffin records the reactions of the people of Taunton from the time the news that the duke is on his way reaches them until Lord Feversham, Colonel Kirke, and Lord Jeffreys, the lord chief justice, finish their bloody deeds. Griffin dramatizes those who pay the price of treason with some effectiveness:

"Not vor ye'r awn, but our zakes!" she exclaimed. "Dwon't ye be zaw desperd unveelin', Teddy. Ax porden, won't ye, Teddy, vor yerzel; an' our dear lads—won't ye save 'em, husband?"

"Naw, I won't thaw," cried the man: "I zed I war ready ta die vor Monmouth, an' I'll stick to it."

"Bit our bways, Teddy!—shall tha niver cum whim any moor?—you dwon't thenk o' them!"

"Ease, but I do thaw—God will take care of 'em. Better vor 'em to have a dead true man than a living turn-qut vor their vather."

So saying, and feeling vexed at importunities that weakened his resolution, he flung her from him with impatience and prepared to meet his fate.[7]

Teddy's blind allegiance and ultimate sacrifice is Griffin's admonition to his readers: beware of any leader who would breach peace and union, morality and law.

The somberness of the duke's progress had to be lightened occasionally with humor, and Griffin's Morty and Shamus Delaney are called upon for this purpose. Still smarting from the memories of the brutalities of "the old thief Cromwell," the brothers leave their Limerick home and family with the understanding that in four years' time they will return on Easter Sunday after having made their fortunes. Griffin's lesson is apparent: as his story ends with Morty and Shamus safely reunited with their family, the year is 1689. Their story of events in England of four years past is eminently appropriate, for in 1689 James II, overthrown by his Calvinist son-in-law, William of Orange, landed in Ireland with an army, only to be defeated on July 1, 1690, by William III.

Their comedy unfolds in scenes like the following in which Captain Shamus Delaney in Monmouth's service briefs his volunteers:

"Well, I see ye're all here, exceptin' those that's absent. Well, then, fall in, fall in, an' much good may it do ye! An' now attind to my ordhers, an' mind 'em well. Every man is to fight, an' nobody is to run; that's plain enough. Secondly, any man that wants arms, is to fight hard *for* 'em first, an' to fight *with* 'em at his aise afther. Thirdly, any booty whatsomever that any o' ye may take in the war, such as goold rings, watches, sails, valuable clothing, an' the likes—but above all things, money—ye're to bring it all to me. Do you hear me?"

"Ay, ay, ay!"

"Very well. Because I'm captain, ye know, an' best judge how it ought to be divided. For it is one o' the maxims of war, that it's the part o' the common sodgers for to fight, an' for the ladin' officers for to have all the call to the booty an' the likes, how 'tis to be shared, an' what's to be done with it. Do ye hear?"

"Ay, ay!" (*D*, 166)

Shamus and Morty, once again on Irish soil and about to join their family on Easter Sunday, view the ruins of their neighborhood on the road to Limerick. Morty addresses his brother:

"Tis an admiration," continued the traveller, "that they left the hill itself there. There's no use in talkin', Shamus, but these English is makin' a band of us intirely. There's Castle-Connel batthered to bits, an' Castle-Throy knocked to tatthers; an' not a spot that we remember far or near, that was ever good for anything, but what's in *smithereens*. I don't know, from Adam, what'll be the end of it."

"Ah, man," said his companion, "if you were to be frettin' yourself that way about everything conthrairy that happens in the world, you never would have a day's pace of quit'ness. Sure, how can we help it if they're batthered itself? Sure tisn't we could keep 'em up." (*D*, 442–43)

Their story of service to Monmouth and Kirke, coming two years before the disaster of the Treaty of Limerick with its horrendous system of religious persecution, would have been prophetic in terms of any Irish support of James once William proved himself master of England. Griffin's point is clear: Ireland neither must wait for peace, as Morty suggests, nor contest for it. Her hope for the future is working through clear lines of authority determined by a whole and united people.

The note of moderation in politics Griffin wished to convey in *The Duke of Monmouth* for Ireland's immediate future would have been lost to his readers, even with a preface similar to the one he supplied for *The Invasion* in which he pompously outlined his patriotic role. *The Duke of Monmouth*'s plot is feeble and anticlimactic. Characters think and act solely in terms of their political feelings. As crucial as Monmouth's advance is to the lives of the Fullartons and the Kingslys, it simply does not generate human response in characters like Aquila Fullarton who can calmly crochet a handkerchief to present to the duke while the lives of those most dear to her are threatened. Griffin strove to show the effects of excessive patriotism, but he explained little of the human condition which caused it. What he is successful in demonstrating is the shock of war upon the people of Taunton and Bridgewater. What he conjures is the memory of what befell the Irish people after the fall of Limerick in 1691. Dryden's words written in 1681 were true for Griffin in 1836 and speak volumes for today: " . . . the People have a Right Supreme/To make their Kings; for Kings are made for them."[8] Daniel O'Connell, as great a "king" as he certainly was, lost his crown when he lost sight of what the people needed before he fulfilled his boast of repeal of the Act of Union. At the time of this writing Griffin himself was seeking order, authority, balance, perspective in his life, and he felt his countrymen should do the same. For all of his efforts, his book was not reviewed by the *Literary Gazette*, the most influential review of his time, but in 1844, when O'Connell's cause collapsed and the Liberator was jailed for a year, an unsigned review of the biography, *The Invasion*, and *Gisippus* called *The Duke*

of Monmouth "a signal failure . . . by many degrees below medioc-
rity."[9] Griffin's political analogies passed unrecognized and the
"romance" of his story quite justifiably was condemned.

V   Talis Qualis; or, Tales of the Jury Room: *Summary and Analysis*

Gerald did not inform William or Daniel, with whom he was living
in George Street, Limerick, of his plans for religious retirement until
a few days before his departure for Dublin on September 7, 1838. He
had given William the *Gisippus* manuscript, and in all likelihood,
William saw to the publication of *Talis Qualis* in the first collected
edition of his brother's works in 1842–1843.

Talis Qualis adds little to the thesis that a moral paralysis ended
Griffin's art, but it does indicate what he did not want to appear in
print at this time. Some of what he suppressed is provocative and brilliant while the juryroom structure is respectable. William seems wholly
justified in having offered it to the public.

"The Prophecy," the tale of the eleventh juror, establishes the time
in which these tales supposedly are being told—1831. It is the year that
the "Rockites, Lady Clare Boys, White Boys, Terry Alts, the agrarian
secret societies at large were armed and embattled against the landlords and the forces of law and order,"[10] and within its own highly
dramatic, Carletonesque fashion this tale outlines the violence and misery inflicted by British troops and peasant guerrilla bands upon the
people of Clare during the agrarian wars raging in the period 1831 to
1838. By far the best tale of the series, "The Prophecy" represents Griffin's skill in creating social verisimilitude; however, at this time he
rejected any element in his writing which might have produced controversy. He was content with the political analogies of *The Invasion*
and *The Duke of Monmouth,* with the gentle, healing qualities in the
satire of *Tales of My Neighbourhood.* The times, he believed, forbade
any stronger elements of social criticism, and so *Talis Qualis* remained
unpublished in his lifetime.

The arrival of an Englishman in Cork during the week of the assizes
suggests Griffin's intention in the light satire that follows: with an outsider looking in, some sense of objectivity may be conveyed to Irishmen
who, more through an inherent, defensive mistrust of the law than an
inclination for mischief and mayhem, tend to explode in debate or to
find themselves immersed in some other equally destructive exercise,
thus forgetting the purpose before them—the pursuit of justice
through the calm and thorough execution of the law. The year is 1831,

some time within the Lenten period, but judging from the politically charged air of the coffeehouse into which the stranger strolls, the spirit of redemption is conspicuously absent as Griffin makes a point about political parties who keep society in an uproar even during the holy season. The Englishman is impressed immediately with the irrational speech of the different party members who are attempting to discuss the case that is to be tried that day involving a breach of promise to marry, with the plaintiff and the defendant representing, respectively, the two opposing political parties which seem to be the instigators of the entire affair.

His curiosity considerably aroused following the trial, the Englishman visits the jury room only to be forced to take cover in the turf closet lest he be embarrassed by the jurymen who are now filing into the small chamber. The twelve jurors have been confined to deliberation until they reach a verdict in the case of the unfortunate lovers, but rather than settling down to the business at hand, under the sponsorship of the foreman, an evening of storytelling is set in progress with each man having to tell one tale and sing one song at its conclusion. A forfeiture of one shilling is exacted against any juryman who fails to entertain with a song. Thus is justice halted, the foreigner trapped, and the tales begun.

Calm, not controversy, was the growing concern of the writer who was preparing his life for service to God. Hence, the ingredients of his juror's tales proved to be objectionable and were put aside. For example, in "The Mistake," the fourth juror's tale, satire, murder, and infidelity combine for amusement but hardly for edification. The story itself is delightful in its presentation of Phelim O'Rourke's attempts to eliminate his shrew of a wife Anty by placing her in the care of the hospital and the "murthering profession" so that he may have his beloved Maggy Fitzgerald. Father John Magrath in "Drink, My Brother" is the single instance in Griffin's writing in which a priest has a central role. Father Magrath's "independent, unyielding, and foreign" character make him a figure more likely to draw criticism than admiration for his attempts to lead his congregation into the light of the nineteenth century. Griffin was able to write the story of an enlightened priest fighting the complacency and ignorance of his parish, but he was unwilling to publish it. The seventh juror's tale, "McEneiry, The Covetous," a folktale, satirizes the classes and customs of ancient bards while "Mr. Tibbot O'Leary, the Curious of Chore Abbey" is Griffin's satirical appraisal of antiquarians. Both tales attacked institutions cherished by Irishmen, and Griffin wisely refrained from introducing them in these heated times. The ninth juror's tale, "The Lame Tailor of Macel," is a feeble conveyance for the old Griffin theme of the supremacy of Christian education over pagan learning. "Antrim Jack, and His General" is skillfully written and possesses excitement and color in the figures of O'Dwyer, the Wicklow rebel, and his devoted follower Jack, a deserter from the British army; but Griffin considered the actions of these heroic outlaws unacceptable for publication in view of the troubled 1830s.

"The Prophecy," the eleventh juror's tale, approaches the beauty and realism of Banim's best work, *Crohoore of the Bill-Hook*. It depicts graphically the victimization of the peasants by the Terry Alts, their own people, and the British troops. Posing no solution, preaching no sermon, it simply presents the stark facts of the brutalities involved in the agrarian civil war taking place in Clare in the early 1830s.

Morris Moran suffers the persecution of Will Wiley, in "The Prophecy," from the moment that Morris as a boy withstands the horrible discovery, from the lips of an old hag and in the midst of a family fireside entertainment, that he is doomed to hang. Morris's friend Peter Nocten scoffs at the prophecy and so draws the wrath of the old woman who sees his fate marked clearly in the sign she draws on the cabin's floor before the hearth—a coffin with the initials P. N. upon it. Will Wiley, the hunchback, lives for the pleasure of tormenting his neighbors, and now Morris and Peter become his prey and the fulfillment of the prophecy, his ambition.

Will Wiley is not an informer until his people accuse him of being one. In that moment, the hunchback chooses, as part of his revenge, to send British soldiers to the door of Peter Nocten, who has been forced from his land for voting against his landlord in the Clare elections of 1828 and is now barely surviving in a mud cabin by the side of a road with the last member of his family, his dying daughter. Peter tells Morris what happened upon that occasion:

"Night and day, I watched the little craythur, and got medicine for her, and gev her goat's milk by the Docthor's orders, and every whole happorth the neighbours said was good for her; but 'twas all of no avail. She grew worse and worse, and had heavy pasperations on her, and was talking wild-like in her sleep at night, and the cough and the pain in the side wor killen. If you were only to see her, Morris, the little craythur looken up at me, after a violent fit, 'twould go to your very heart. 'I wish I was in Heaven daddy,' she used to say sometimes, and her lip tremblin, for 'then I'd have no more pain!' Well why, she grew so bad at last, I was obliged to give up the work and sit by the sop of straw constant, minding her, not knowen the moment she'd daw

the breath. As I was watching this way last night, sometimes raising and settling her up when the oppression 'ud come on her, sometimes fixing the sods
closer in the covering over her head, for the weather was wet and stormy, I
thought I heard the sound of footsteps, like the tramp of sodgers between the
gusts. I found I was right enough, for in a few minutes the shed in which we
lay was surrounded, the door was thrown in, and a police officer stoopen
down, desired me to come out and surrender. He laughed, the ruffian, when
I axed him what it was I done to make a prison of me, sayen I'd know shortly
to my cost; and when I pointed to my dying little girl, and begged of him to
lave me, until I'd get one of the neighbours to mind her in the morning, he
presented a pistol, and swore he'd shoot me unless I came out without delay.
I grew wild to think of laving the little craythur to die alone, and slipping the
handle of a spade behind me, I pretended I was comen to give myself up—
he drew back to let me pass, when suddenly I darted out, and was lost in the
pitchy darkness of the night; some of 'em fired after me, and others followed
by the sound of my steps. But when I thought they were a little asunder, I
stopped on a sudden and stretched the first that come up, wid a blow of the
spade-tree. Three more I sarved in the same way, and the rest thought it
better for 'em to give up the hunt. I got back again to my little darlen before
long, and I'd give a hundred lives if I had 'em, for the one look she gev me,
when I come into her. Young as she was, she understood all that happened to
me, and put out her little mouth to kiss me, as I sat down by the bed. But her
lips were cold, and the lamp of death was on her forehead and her eyes were
glazen. I lifted her off the straw, wrapped the blanket about her and thanks
be to God, she died in my arms. I was as happy a most at the mercy, as if
they were all again brought back to me. The sodgers were with me soon after,
horse, foot and police, but *I had nothing now to fight for*—I walked out of
the shed quiet and asy—held my hands stretched for the hand-cuffs, and
never med complaint more."[11]

So upset about the horrors of the times in Clare was Griffin that when
he wrote to Lydia Fisher on March 31, 1833, he inadvertently renamed
the "Whiteboys," one of the secret agrarian guerrilla societies: "Oh,
dear L——— [Lydia], why didn't you make the Whitefeet behave
themselves? They have almost made me ashamed of my country . . .
when I hear of one murder after another committed by these unhappy
wretches."[12]

The last tale is that of the Englishman who has been detected and
led into the evening's entertainment. The gentleman is both daring and
resourceful in his selection: "The Raven's Nest" concerns the strife
between the Geraldines and the Kildares immediately following the
accession of Henry VII in 1485, and its best scene is reminiscent of
John Donne's "Satyre I" in which the poet unmercifully flays courtiers.

In "The Raven's Nest" the Munster and Ulster heroes, the Geraldines and the O'Neills, are satirized by Sir Ulick Kildare for their crudities at a Dublin ball. However, the Geraldines emerge heroically against the forces of the earl of Kildare as peace is finally restored. The Englishman has made his point for both sides of the Irish Sea, for his "captors" and himself: ironically and felicitously, his survival is owed to his willingness to accept his situation and to work within it for the most meaningful understandings of the paradoxical masses of eight million Irishmen. *Talis Qualis* concludes the following day in court as the curious visitor learns amid the uproar of laughter in the courtroom that the lovers escaped the tentacles of their political parties by eloping at five o'clock that morning.

In this collection, offered to Griffin's readers two years after his death, there appears sufficient internal evidence to indicate that this writer was concerned always about the effects his writing might have upon his reading public. He wished to offend no one; he wanted peace for his people. His staunch conservatism is felt in all his preachments. It was with this kind of a conscience that he left for the Christian Brothers' seminary in Cork in September, 1838.

CHAPTER 8

Conclusion

"REASONS for My Faith," written by Gerald Griffin in 1829 and published for the first time thirty-eight years after his death in the *Irish Monthly*,[1] had been in the keeping of one of his fellow brothers at the Cork Monastery. The editor informs his reader that the period "of negligence and wavering which he here describes must be confined to the early part of his miserable struggles in London."[2] Not entirely, for the year 1829 was a precipitous one for Griffin. His fame as the author of *The Collegians* made him uneasy and so did his new friendship with Lydia Fisher.

In this confession he wrote of London during the years 1823 to 1827: "In my days of scepticism and neglect all my natural dispositions flowed into one selfish channel. Pride made me sensitive, and accordingly I quarrelled with my best friends. Ambition made me selfish, and I neglected my duty to my natural relatives and superiors."[3] Daniel Griffin's biography of his brother confirms this much, but it does not include the following: "Passion made me luxurious, and my days were sensual and irregular. Selfishness made me suspicious, and I suspected evil where I saw virtue."[4] Passion and sensuality were not a part of his London years: they followed his triumph with *The Collegians*. "Long was it," he wrote, "even after I fully believed, before I could obtain anything like a solid consolation, or internal assurance of the foregiveness of my God, and sincerity obliges me to confess again that fear, perhaps entirely selfish, was the first motive of my conversion to religion, and the means of driving me back to the bosom of my Church."[5]

Contrition through fear is imperfect sorrow in the eyes of his church but it is sufficient. What this "sinner" had to do was to perfect his sorrow for his failings, and his writing became one means for accomplishing this purpose. "Reasons for My Faith" was a prologue for all his future work. It was a declaration that he was a free soul in the service of his God and his country, one who would try to write "perfectly moral" books. If he needed a "long" time to win consolation for his lapse of faith in London, he needed nine years to prepare himself for a monastic life.

Anglo-Irish prose began with writers like Edgeworth, Banim, and Griffin, but only Griffin attempted to justify all he wrote in terms of moral instruction. Perhaps his readers were less afraid of either a spiritual or a physical death than this earnest moralist, or, perhaps, as Arland Ussher says, an "Irishman cannot really take morality seriously, as a good in itself like religion or beauty; for him it is either the book of the rules for getting to heaven, or a matter of personal fastidiousness."[6] In either case, Griffin's success and achievement ended as soon as it began. As an artist he never was able to transcend the deepest significance of the Judeo-Christian concept of man's fall.

Griffin's lasting literary contribution is *The Collegians* and the recreation of a Munster neighborhood. Inextricably a part of this creation was his commitment to the teachings of the Roman Catholic Church which he imposed upon his readers, thus making any appreciation of his work in his time and today somewhat difficult. In the fifty to one hundred years that separates Griffin from writers like Synge, Joyce, O'Faolain, and Brian Moore, Griffin appears more the priest ready with direct counseling, one eager to set problems of the soul aright rather than to shed any light upon the passions which created his character's predicament. More accessible to readers who understand his purpose in writing, Griffin enters the world of reprinted editions as a fine Irish Catholic regionalist whose life was analogous to that of his country: emerging as an artist at a time when his people were being lead to religious freedom, Griffin finally turned from art in writing to art in Christian living.

That Griffin was read throughout the nineteenth century is confirmed by the many editions of his works published in Ireland and America as late as the 1880s. And today, *The Collegians* is sold in book shops in Dublin while school children in counties Clare and Limerick know its story well.

Yeats included *The Collegians* in his list of the best Irish books,[7] and Padraic Colum[8] and Frank O'Connor[9] continue the recognition of one of the world's first regionalists, one who, with Scott and Turgenev, followed the example of Maria Edgeworth, creator of regionalism in Western literature.[10]

That such novelists as Graham Greene, Brian Moore, Iris Murdoch, and Evelyn Waugh were influenced by Griffin's writings is not improbable. That these writers, among others, constitute a Roman Catholic tradition in the novel, a tradition of writing stories espousing the teaching of the Catholic Church, seems quite apparent to the reader. And that this tradition began in Ireland with Gerald Griffin is to his credit.

Notes and References

Preface

1. R. B. McDowell, *Irish Public Opinion in the Eighteenth Century: 1750–1800* (London: Transatlantic Arts, 1944), p. 123.
2. "Gerald Griffin As a Christian Brother," in *The Christian Brothers' Publication: Annual Education Record* (1891), p. 307.
3. Daniel Griffin, *The Life of Gerald Griffin By His Brother*, 2d ed. (Dublin: James Duffy, 1872), p. 397.
4. Correspondence from John Cronin to Robert Davis.
5. Griffin, *Life*, pp. 273–74.
6. Review of the biography, *The Invasion*, and *Gisippus*, *Dublin Review*, 16, no. 32 (March, June, 1844), 281–307.
7. Thomas Flanagan, *The Irish Novelists: 1800–1850* (New York: Columbia University Press, 1959), p. 46.

Chapter One

1. Ethel Mannin, *Two Studies in Integrity: Gerald Griffin and the Reverend Francis Mohoney ('Father Prout')* (New York: G. P. Putnam's Sons, 1954), p. 109.
2. *The Poetical and Dramatic Works of Gerald Griffin* (Dublin: James Duffy, n.d.), p. 206.
3. M. Mohoney, "Limerick and Gerald Griffin," *North Munster Antiquarian Journal*, 2 (1940–1941), 4.
4. Mohoney, p. 6.
5. Patrick John Dowling, *The Hedge Schools of Ireland* (London: Longmans, Green, 1935), p. 134.
6. Flanagan, pp. 171–72.
7. Mannin, p. 55.
8. Griffin, *Life*, p. 148.
9. *The Journal of Sir Walter Scott* (New York: Harper, 1890), II, 143.
10. Griffin, *Life*, p. 224.
11. Ibid., pp. 235–36.
12. Ibid., p. 238.

13. Ibid., p. 178.

14. Ibid., p. 310.

15. Ibid., pp. 246–47.

16. Ibid., p. 248.

17. Lydia Jane Fisher, *Letters from the Kingdom of Kerry in the Year 1845* (Dublin: Webb and Chapman, 1847), p. 88.

18. Ibid., p. 95.

19. Griffin, *Life*, pp. 396–97.

20. Mannin, p. 92.

21. Samuel Carter Hall, *A Book of Memories of Great Men and Women of the Age, from Personal Acquaintance* (London: Virtue, 1871), p. 230.

22. Mannin, p. 120.

23. Denis Gwynn, *The Struggle for Catholic Emancipation* (London: Longmans, Green, 1928), p. xxi.

24. Thomas H. D. Mohoney, *Edmund Burke and Ireland* (Cambridge: Harvard University Press, 1960), p. 317.

Chapter Two

1. Edmund Spenser, *A View of the Present State of Ireland*, ed. W. L. Renwick (Oxford: Clarendon Press, 1970), p. 5.

2. *The English in Ireland in the Eighteenth Century* (London: Longmans, Green, 1874), II, 7.

3. Constantia Maxwell, *Country and Town in Ireland Under the Georges* (Dundalk: W. Tempest, 1949), p. 18.

4. David H. Green, *An Anthology of Irish Literature* (New York: Random House, 1954), pp. xxix–xxx.

5. Maureen Wall, "The Rise of a Catholic Middle Class in Eighteenth Century Ireland," *Irish Historical Studies*, 11, no. 42 (September, 1958); reprinted in Irish Studies History Series, no. 2, from the American Committee for Irish Studies (Chicago: University of Chicago Press, 1971), p. 97.

6. W. E. H. Lecky, *Leaders of Public Opinion in Ireland* (London: Longmans, Green, 1872), pp. 8–10.

7. Ibid., p. 12.

8. Mohoney, *Edmund Burke*, pp. 212–13.

9. Thomas N. Brown, "Nationalism and the Irish Peasant," *Review of Politics*, 15, no. 4 (April, 1971); reprinted in Irish Studies History Series, no. 1, from the American Committee for Irish Studies (Chicago: University of Chicago Press, 1971), p. 413.

10. Daniel Corkery, *The Hidden Ireland* (Dublin: M. H. Gill, 1924), pp. 37–38.

11. Louis A. Landa, *Swift and the Church of Ireland* (Oxford: Clarendon Press, 1954), p. 100.

12. Stephen Lucius Gwynn, *Henry Grattan and His Times* (1939; reprint ed. Westport: Greenwood Press, 1971), p. 126.

13. Ibid., p. 48.

14. Mohoney, *Edmund Burke*, p. 275.

15. M. J. MacManis, *Irish Cavalcade: 1550–1850* (London: Macmillan, 1939), p. 221.

16. Brown, p. 436.

Chapter Three

1. Griffin, *Life*, p. 99.

2. *The Poetical and Dramatic Works of Gerald Griffin*, p. 386.

3. Ibid., p. 392.

4. Mannin, p. 132.

5. "The Dramatic Writers of Ireland," *Dublin University Magazine*, 46, no. 275 (1855), 565.

6. Griffin, *Life*, p. 170.

7. Ibid., p. 142.

8. "Gerald Griffin," *Catholic World*, 2 (1870), 401.

9. Griffin, *Life*, p. 197.

10. Flanagan, p. 176.

11. Gerald Griffin, *Holland-tide* (Dublin: Saunders and Otley, 1857), p. 3–4; hereafter cited in the text as *H*.

12. "Gerald Griffin As A Christian Brother," p. 310.

Chapter Four

1. Flanagan, p. 171.

2. Griffin, *Life*, p. 190.

3. Ibid., p. 200.

4. Gerald Griffin, *Tales of the Munster Festivals* (London: Maxwell & Co., 1842), p. 7: hereafter cited in the text as *T*.

Chapter Five

1. Griffin, *Life*, p. 220.

2. Scott acknowledged his indebtedness for the story of Helen Walker in the "Introduction" to his text, dated, at Abbotsford, April 1, 1830. He had formerly published in the preface to the *Cronicles of the Canongate* (1827), "that he received from an anonymous correspondent an account of the incident upon which the following story is founded." The preceding information is taken from Scott's *The Heart of Midlothian* (1818; reprint ed. London: J. M. Dent, 1956), pp. 3–8.

3. Gerald Griffin, *The Collegians* (1829: reprint ed. Dublin: Talbot Press, Ltd., 1944), p. 120; hereafter cited in the text as *C*.

4. Flanagan, p. 222.

5. Griffin, *Life*, p. 225.

6. Aubrey De Vere, "Gerald Griffin," in *Recollections of Aubrey De Vere* (London: E. Arnold, 1897), p. 31.

7. Griffin, *Life*, p. 360.

8. Henry Fielding, *Amelia* (1751; reprint ed. London: J. M. Dent, 1962), II, 62.

9. Maria Edgeworth, *Castle Rackrent* (1800; reprint ed., London: Oxford University Press, 1964), pp. 56–57.

10. Scott, *The Heart of Midlothian*, p. 326.

11. John Banim, *Crohoore of the Bill-Hook* (London: W. Simpkin and R. Marshall, 1825), pp. 181–82.

12. Ibid., pp. 185–86.

13. Ibid., p. 197.

14. Fielding, I, 4.

Chapter Six

1. Griffin, *Life*, p. 231.

2. J. C. Beckett, *The Making of Modern Ireland: 1603–1923* (New York: Knopf, 1966), p. 258.

3. Ibid., p. 258.

4. *The Christian Physiologist* (London: E. Bull, 1830).

5. Ibid., p. 7.

6. Ibid., p. 63.

7. Griffin, *Life*, p. 275.

8. Gerald Griffin, *The Invasion* (Dublin: James Duffy, n.d.), p. 4; hereafter cited in the text as *I*.

9. "Gerald Griffin's Common-Place Book A," *Eire-Ireland*, 4, no. 3 (1969), 37.

10. "Literature and Biography," in *Relations of Literary Study: Essays on Interdisciplinary Contributions*, ed. James Thorpe (New York, 1967), pp. 62–63.

Chapter Seven

1. Gerald Griffin, *Tales of My Neighbourhood* (London: Saunders and Otley, 1835), I, 71: hereafter cited in the text as *N*.

2. Griffin, *Life*, p. 315.

3. John Dryden, *The Poems and Fables of John Dryden*, ed. James Kinsley (London: Oxford University Press, 1962), p. 189.

4. Ibid., p. 209.

5. Beckett, pp. 306–7.

6. Sir George Clark, *The Later Stuarts: 1660–1714* (Oxford: Clarendon Press, 1934), pp. 119–20.

7. Gerald Griffin, *The Duke of Monmouth* (New York: James Duffy, 1886), p. 243; hereafter cited in the text as *D*.

8. Dryden, p. 200.

9. *Dublin Review*, 16, no. 32 (March, June 1844), 291–92.

10. Alf MacLocklainn, "Social Life in County Clare, 1800–1850," *Irish University Review: A Journal of Irish Studies*, 2, no. 1 (1972), 69–70.

11. Gerald Griffin, *Talis Qualis; or, Tales of the Jury Room* (London: Maxwell, 1842), pp. 452–53.

12. Griffin, *Life*, p. 314.

Chapter Eight

1. (March, 1878), 148–57.

2. Ibid., p. 148.

3. Ibid., p 154.

4. Ibid.

5. Ibid., p. 155.

6. *The Face and Mind of Ireland* (New York: Devin-Adair, 1950), p. 138.

7. W. B. Yeats, "Irish National Literature, IV: A List of the Best Irish Books," in *Uncollected Prose by W. B. Yeats*, ed. John P. Frayne, vol. 1 (New York: Columbia University Press, 1970), pp. 382–87.

8. From the introduction, to *The Collegians* (Dublin: Talbot Press Limited, 1944), p. xv.

9. *A Short History of Irish Literature: A Backward Look* (New York: G. P. Putnam's Sons, 1967), p. 147.

10. James Newcomer, *Maria Edgeworth the Novelist* (Fort Worth, Texas: Christian University Press, 1967), p. 28.

Selected Bibliography

PRIMARY SOURCES

Holland-tide; or Munster Popular Tales. London: Saunders and Otley, 1827.
Tales of the Munster Festivals. London: Saunders and Otley, 1827.
The Collegians. London: Saunders and Otley, 1829.
The Christian Physiologist: Tales Illustrative of the Five Senses. London: E. Bull, 1830.
The Rivals and Tracy's Ambition. London: Saunders and Otley, 1830.
The Invasion. London: Saunders and Otley, 1832.
Tales of My Neighbourhood. London: Saunders and Otley, 1835.
The Duke of Monmouth. London: R. Bentley, 1836.
Gisippus. London: Maxwell, 1842.
Talis Qualis; or, Tales of the Jury Room. London: Maxwell, 1842.
Poetical Works. London: Simpkin and Marshall, 1843.
"Reasons for My Faith." *Irish Monthly,* 6 (1878), 148–57.

SECONDARY SOURCES

ANON. "The Dramatic Writers of Ireland." *Dublin University Magazine,* 46, no. 275 (1855), 565. While noting the lack of female interest in *Gisippus,* this early reviewer, who may have seen Macready in the title role in 1842 in Drury Lane, regrets that so promising a playwright failed to receive sufficient encouragement at the early age of twenty.
ANON. "Gerald Griffin." *Catholic World,* 2 (1870), 398–411. A general review of Griffin's biography with assurances from relatives and friends of the author that his "practical duties of faith" did not lapse during his London trials.
ANON. "Gerald Griffin As a Christian Brother." In *The Christian Brothers' Publication:—Annual Education Record* (1891), pp. 305–19. Notes about Griffin as a Christian Brother together with glimpses into the past.
ANON. Review of the biography, *The Invasion,* and *Gisippus. Dublin Review,* 16, no. 32 (March, June, 1844), 281–307. Griffin in a contemporary literary perspective. A salute to his "simple and natural reality," his contribution to true Irish nationality in literature.

BANIM, JOHN. *Crohoore of the Bill-Hook*. London: W. Simpkin and R. Marshall, 1825. A masterpiece of peasant realities in eighteenth-century Leinster.

BECKETT, J. C. *The Making of Modern Ireland: 1603–1923*. New York: Knopf, 1966. Ireland today better understood through this brilliant summary and commentary.

BROWN, THOMAS W. "Nationalism and the Irish Peasant: 1800–1848." *Review of Politics*, 15, no. 4 (April, 1971). Reprinted in Irish Studies History Series, no. 1, from the American Committee for Irish Studies (Chicago: University of Chicago Press, 1971). Fine commentary on the rise of "young Ireland."

CLARK, SIR GEORGE. *The Later Stuarts: 1660–1714*. Oxford: Clarendon Press, 1934. In light of this history, Griffin's town scenes in *The Duke of Monmouth* seem more credible.

CORKERY, DANIEL. *The Hidden Ireland*. Dublin: M. H. Gill, 1924. The history and value of eighteenth-century Munster Gaelic poetry.

CRONIN, JOHN. "Gerald Griffin and the Collegians: A Reconsideration." *University Review*, 5 (1968), 57–63. A successful attempt to rescue Griffin's image from nineteenth-century distortions.

———. "Gerald Griffin's Common-Place Book A." *Éire-Ireland*, 4, no. 3 (1969), 22–37. Griffin's intense interest and dedication to writing *The Invasion* revealed in this source.

———. "Gerald Griffin, Dedalus *Manqué*." *Studies*, 58 (1969), 267–78. The rationale here is that Griffin failed, understandably, because of "history and circumstance." Plus, a diptych of Joyce and Griffin.

———. "Gerald Griffin: A Forgotten Novel." *Éire-Ireland*, 5 (1970), 32–39. Not to be forgotten: this "satiric realism and comic force" of *Adventures of an Irish Giant*.

———. "The Passionate Perfectionist." *Hibernia*, 36, (March, 1971), 16. A brief testimonial.

DE VERE, AUBREY. "Gerald Griffin." In *Recollections of Aubrey De Vere*. London: E. Arnold, 1897. pp. 27–33. Fully expected Griffin to become the Scott of Ireland.

DOWLING, PATRICK JOHN. *The Hedge Schools of Ireland*. London: Longmans, Green, 1935. Richard McElligott and T. M. O'Brien, two of Griffin's teachers, contrasted in this history of a once vital Irish institution.

DRYDEN, JOHN. *The Poems and Fables of John Dryden*. Edited by James Kinsley. London: Oxford University Press, 1962. The tenets of this great Augustan preside over much of what Griffin wrote on the subjects of authority and rule.

EDEL, LEON. "Literature and Biography." In *Relations of Literary Study: Essays on Interdisciplinary Contributions*, edited by James Thorpe, pp. 62–63. New York: Modern Language Association of America, 1967. Preeminent authority for the thesis that Griffin sounded his decision to quit art in his writing.

EDGEWORTH, MARIA. *Castle Rackrent.* 1800; reprint ed., London: Oxford University Press, 1964. The begetter of regionalism in literature.

FIELDING, HENRY. *Amelia.* 1751; reprint ed., London: J. M. Dent, 1962. Fielding (as magistrate) and Griffin (as court reporter) intent on social reform in their writing.

FISHER, LYDIA JANE. *Letters from the Kingdom of Kerry in the Year 1845.* Dublin: Webb and Chapman, 1847. Contains a note of profound loss of a "beloved friend."

FLANAGAN, THOMAS. *The Irish Novelists: 1800–1850.* New York: Columbia University Press, 1959. A major contribution in the study of Anglo-Irish literature.

FROUDE, JAMES ANTHONY. *The English in Ireland in the Eighteenth Century.* London: Longmans, Green, 1874. His abuse of things Irish and his advocacy of English imperialism nevertheless publicized many of Ireland's ills.

GREENE, DAVID H. *An Anthology of Irish Literature.* New York: Random House, 1954. An unsurpassed introduction to the literature of Ireland.

GRIFFIN, DANIEL. *The Life of Gerald Griffin By His Brother.* 2d ed. Dublin: James Duffy, 1872. Guarded, sketchy yet essential moments appear.

GWYNN, DENIS. *The Struggle for Catholic Emancipation.* London: Longmans, Green, 1928. The central issue of the first three decades of the nineteenth century compressed.

GWYNN, STEPHEN LUCIUS. *Henry Grattan and His Times.* 1939; reprint ed., Westport: Greenwood Press, 1971. The rise and fall of this significant leader of the Anglo-Irish Ascendancy brilliantly traced for the general reader.

HALL, SAMUEL CARTER. *A Book of Memories of Great Men and Women of the Age, from Personal Acquaintance.* London: Virtue, 1871. Two years before he entered the order of the Christian Brothers Griffin condemned his novels as sins.

LANDA, LOUIS A. *Swift and the Church of Ireland.* Oxford: Clarendon Press, 1954. A brilliant treatment of Swift's role as master of an enduring Anglican establishment.

LECKY, W. E. H. *Leaders of Public Opinion in Ireland.* London: Longmans, Green, 1872. Very positive feelings about the state of Ireland explained in terms of the work of Swift, Flood, Grattan, and O'Connell.

MC DOWELL, R. B. *Irish Public Opinion in the Eighteenth Century: 1750–1800.* London: Transatlantic Arts, 1944. Subservient Irish politics until an excluded Catholic majority begins its siege.

MACLOCKLAINN, ALF. "Social Life in County Clare, 1800–1850." *Irish University Review: A Journal of Irish Studies,* 2, no. 1 (1972), 55–78. A view of Clare's "vernacular culture."

MACMANUS, M. J. *Irish Cavalcade: 1550–1850.* London: Macmillan, 1939. An eclectic's repository of great moments in Irish history.

MANNIN, ETHEL. *Two Studies in Integrity: Gerald Griffin and the Reverend Francis Mohoney ('Father Prout').* New York: G. P. Putnam, 1954. Contains correspondence not presented in biography.

MAXWELL, CONSTANTIA. *Country and Town in Ireland Under the Georges.* Dundalk: W. Tempest, 1949. A good deal of descriptive material accompanied by a fine bibliography.

MOHONEY, M. "Limerick and Gerald Griffin." *North Munster Antiquarian Journal,* 2 (1940–1941), 4. Griffin's ancestors traced back to chiefs and large freeholders until Cromwellian Plantation.

MOHONEY, THOMAS H. D. *Edmund Burke and Ireland.* Cambridge: Harvard University Press, 1960. A champion of justice for the Irish.

NEWCOMER, JAMES. *Maria Edgeworth the Novelist, 1767–1849: A Bicentennial Study.* Forth Worth: Texas Christian University Press, 1967. A competent reconsideration of one of Ireland's first novelists.

SCOTT, SIR WALTER. *The Heart of Midlothian,* 1818; reprint ed., London: J. M. Dent, 1956. Griffin's master.

———. *The Journal of Sir Walter Scott.* New York: Harper, 1890. II, 143. A shrewd and just appraisal of Griffin's worth based on *Tales of the Munster Festivals.*

SPENSER, EDMUND. *A View of the Present State of Ireland.* Edited by W. L. Renwick. Oxford: Clarendon Press, 1970. A poet's "official opinion" on a tumultuous time in Irish and English affiars.

USSHER, ARLAND. *The Face and Mind of Ireland.* New York: Devin-Adair, 1950. Who Irishmen are by a descendant of the Ascendancy.

WALL, MAUREEN. "The Rise of a Catholic Middle Class in Eighteenth Century Ireland." *Irish Historical Studies,* 11, no. 42 (September, 1958). Reprinted in Irish Studies History Series, no. 2, from the American Committee for Irish Studies (Chicago: University of Chicago, 1971). Catholic landed proprietors, among other factors, contributed to the creation of a powerful Catholic middle class.

YEATS, WILLIAM BUTLER. "Irish National Literature, IV: A List of the Best Irish Books." In *Uncollected Prose by W. B. Yeats.* Edited by John P. Frayne. Vol. 1. New York: Columbia University Press, 1970. pp. 382–87. A helpful reference to the poet's pronouncements on things great and small.

Index